D1236610

The Baudelairean Cinema
A Trend within the
American Avant-Garde

Studies in Cinema, No. 8

Diane M. Kirkpatrick, Series Editor

Associate Professor, History of Art
The University of Michigan

Other Titles in This Series

The Baudelairean Cinema
A Trend within the American Avant-Garde

by
Carel Rowe

UMI RESEARCH PRESS
Ann Arbor, Michigan

NMU LIBRARY

Produced and distributed by
UMI Research Press
an imprint of
University Microfilms International
Ann Arbor, Michigan 48106

Library of Congress Cataloging in Publication Data

Rowe, Carel.
  The Baudelairean cinema.

  (Studies in cinema ; no. 8)
  Revision of thesis (Ph.D.)—Northwestern University,
1977.
  Bibliography: p.
  Includes index.
  1. Experimental films—United States—History and
criticism.   I. Title. II. Series.
  PN1995.9.E96R6 1982   791.43'0973   81-16243
  ISBN 0-8357-1268-0   AACR2

For William T. Berkman

Contents

List of Figures

Introduction

In 1972 I organized and produced the first (and last) Lurid Film Festival at Northwestern University. This festival was simply a series of screenings of experimental American films which I had selected for their "underground" notoriety. This event—which was no doubt of rather limited appeal—coincided with and was overshadowed by the annual student spring festivities: "Spring Thing." The audience was made up of bleary-eyed students who had wandered into the Technological Institute auditorium almost by accident, on their way home from their weekend of beer and rock concerts on the shores of Lake Michigan.

By now, one can almost hear the waves of Lake Michigan gently wiping out any residual memory of the violence engendered by the First Lurid Film Festival. Any notoriety which this festival achieved was more the result of diverse audience reactions than a question of film content. A dozen or so males in the audience literally assaulted the locked doors of the projection booth (where I was hiding), demanding box-office refunds and apologies. (In retrospect, it is interesting to note that these men were what we commonly called "jocks"—as opposed to "tech wienies"—quite simply, members of the football team.) The shouting, the demand for refunds, the kicking and pounding of the projection room doors occurred toward the end of the festival, two-thirds of the way into *Flaming Creatures* (1963), a notorious film about a transvestite orgy which I had ordered, unseen, inspired by Susan Sontag's rapturous article.[1]

The exceptional thing about what happened was that on that particular evening, for the first third of the film, the audience had laughed as raucously for *Creatures* as they had for the George Kuchar film which preceded it (*Hold Me While I'm Naked*, 1966); then, suddenly, the crowd grew ugly. Of course, the film's relentless pansexuality bothered them—in content, it quite outstripped even the raunchy rock lyrics they'd been dancing to only hours before. But the aggravation also stemmed from what Andrew Sarris recently called "the hyped-up audience's erotic expectations [which] were disappointed by the film's disconcertingly unaggressive transvestitism."[2]

This minuscule event, one which I am certain only I still recall in detail and with intensity, is responsible for four years of research and application which evolved into this study of the Baudelairean Cinema. In the long run, to me, the major import of the Lurid Film Festival was not simply the audience's reaction to *Flaming Creatures*, but the film itself. I was intrigued by the gulf of perception between the "jocks" and myself. Intrigued by the film's visual qualities and the unique aesthetic it so outrageously displayed, I began to research the effects it had produced at former screenings.

The implications of the lurid incident at my Lurid Film Festival were startling: after reading Jonas Mekas's reports on its reception at the Third International Experimental Film Festival,[3] I realized that I had been lucky to escape without a warrant for obscenity. (The film *had* arrived in "plain brown wrapper" and *had* to be picked up in person by the booker at the airport; but the legal implications were of little interest to me at the time when I was preparing 200 hand-painted posters and enlisting students to help organize projection and ticket-taking.) *Flaming Creatures*, as it turned out, was considered a threat: legally, morally, and sexually.

Mekas reports:

> One of the most revealing experiences I had was during a screening of *Flaming Creatures* to a group of New York writers, upper-class writers who write for money, who expected to see another "blue movie"—I had never met with such violent reactions, such outbursts of uncontrolled anger. Someone was threatening to beat me up. They would have happily sat through a pornographic movie, which they were expecting to see and which the host had promised them that night—but they could not take the fantasies of Jack Smith. *Flaming Creatures* unmasked them and made them face themselves in a way that only art can. That is the difference between pornography and art.[4]

In Europe and America, the effects were identical. This film had some sort of negative potency, a passive virility which threatened "jocks" everywhere. In one of his most vital essays Jonas Mekas described the desperate attempts to screen *Flaming Creatures* in Knokke-le-Zoute in 1964:

> ... there will be conflicting reports about it for years to come, about ... [how] we stormed the Crystal Room and took over the projector, how the lights were cut off, and how I ran to the switchboard room, trying to push off the house detective, holding the door, trying to force the fingers of the bully who was holding the switch.
>
> "People, do you want to see the film?" Barbara Rubin shouted from the projector platform, fighting like a brave general.
>
> "Yes!" answered the people.
>
> It is confusing what went on after that. Much pushing and shouting as the switch changed hands between me and the cop. It was about the time that the Minister of Justice arrived. The riot was getting more and more out of hand. The Minister made an attempt to explain the Belgian law. But when we asked if there was such a law forbidding the showing of films, he said there was no such law. "Then fuck you!" shouted Barbara to the Minister of Justice of Belgium. We made another attempt to project *Flaming Creatures*

right on his face, but the light was cut off again. Later I was told that the Minister of Justice in his speech gave his word that the Belgian laws on this matter will be changed. The morning papers picked up the promise.[5]

After reading this, it became even more of a challenge to decipher the disruptive codes with which *Flaming Creatures* so thoroughly and consistently disturbed its audiences. I longed to understand the menace of this film (which to me, seemed nonthreatening, humorous, and beautiful).

That summer of 1972 I traveled to New York to meet and interview Jack Smith. I spent approximately two and a half months with him, tailing him around town, filming, videotaping and assisting him with his "Sharkbait of Atlantis" slide-shows at the Jane Street Theatre. This, it seemed, was just as far "Underground" as there was to go.

None of my attempts to interview Jack Smith afforded much coherent material, but each encounter provided fresh insights into his exotic, decadent vision. Working with him deepened my admiration for and horror of this "Baudelairean" aesthetic—an aesthetic which Jack always carried with him. His favorite authors were Edgar Allan Poe and Charles Pierre Baudelaire and he quoted from them so frequently that I am certain they were never far from his thoughts. (Unless, of course, he happened to be thinking or talking about the attributes of Maria Montez.) We walked blistering blocks of New York City in search of a perfect rendition of the song "Maria" to suit his slides of Montez and Jon Hall in *Cobra Woman*. (One slide might last through as many as six or seven recorded renditions of the same song.)

Jack always acted lost and confused but knew the city (and it him) perfectly. Often he became totally "lost" in his pursuit of rather contradictory errands; he seemed to move consciously in directions which led toward a succession of receding goals, resulting eventually in several triumphs of disaster. For example, no working record player for the evening's slide show. Or, if a player could not be built out of scraps of electronic-leavings and whatever else could be scavenged on the spot while the audience waited (and eventually left)—no slide show. But it would take all day and the full five hours of performance time to *not* have the slide show.

When not accompanying Jack on these pursuits of frustration, I spent the afternoons in the library of the Anthology Film Archives, researching files and tapes on Jack Smith and having occasional conversations with Jonas Mekas on the difficulty involved in any attempt to communicate verbally with Smith. By that time Smith had once and for all severed relations with Jonas Mekas and all film critics.

Jack's famous quote, "Film critics are writers and they are hostile and uneasy in the presence of a visual phenomenon,"[6] was not to be taken lightly. (I recall sitting through a screening of *Flaming Creatures* with him at the

Anthology Film Archives' "Invisible Theatre"; every so often I sensed a claw-like groping from his seat, his hand would dart through the partition between us. This gesture occurred every time I had turned a page in my notebook. Jack smelled a critic, but due to the hooded structure of the seats, I was able to furtively continue writing, "stealing" his images with words.) I could only hope to maintain friendly relations with Smith as a fellow media artist—and a friend—but my terror of being discovered as a critic/scholar, a "Mekasite," a double agent, mounted.

Jack often spoke of his personal hatred of Jonas Mekas. He was more and more prone to threatening monologues against Mekas while taking coffee breaks in automats in between his endless futile errands around town. Sometimes he resembled an asylum escapee; whenever I mentioned Mekas or the Archives he would fly into a rage, saying, "The whole place is sharkbait." He believed in a Mekas "conspiracy," that a collection of prints had been illegally struck from the Archives' collection. To steal a film, "All it takes is one night in the safe," he would say. Mekas had contributed to the original lab costs, retained his hold on the negative of *Flaming Creatures*, and refused to relinquish it to Smith. One could almost see why. I certainly never questioned Mekas's position in keeping the negative out of Jack's destructive clutches.

It is important to remember that Mekas was the single critical and legal force behind the film; for years he defended *Creatures* in court and in print to protect it from confiscation by the State of New York. If the film had been removed from the Archives' custody, it could have been impounded wherever it was shown. However, Jack continued to demand (writing long, irate, unpublished letters to the *Village Voice*) that Jonas return the film.

I had little idea of Jack's capacity for violence until one fateful night at the Jane Street Theatre. Jonas had smuggled in P. Adams Sitney and Annette Michelson to view the slide show. They sat deep in their seats at the back of the theatre, but someone spotted them and told Jack they were in the audience. Suddenly Jack swung from the balcony onto the stage and rushed up the aisle toward the three critics. He accused me of bringing them to "spy" on his show and banished the four of us from the theatre, screaming that he would murder Jonas if he wrote one word about what he'd seen there that evening.

I never saw Jack Smith again. His slide shows and films, which he so paranoiacally guarded from the "clutches of critics," also seem to have vaporized. After the scene at the Jane Street Theatre, he seemed finally to shut himself off—not only from the critics but from the necessity (or ability) to give performances or make films. His film work has trickled to a standstill since that summer and perhaps no one will have the opportunity, until after his death, to unseal, process, and print the rotting, exposed, and undeveloped scenes from his last (uncompleted) film, *Normal Love.*

Following that summer of bizarre events and encounters, I resolved to do further research on the "disappearing" artist, Jack Smith, and other related American avant-garde filmmakers of the 1960s. My method was to return to the critical writings of Jonas Mekas and to organize my study based on his concept of a "Baudelairean Cinema."[7] I set out to validate Mekas's somewhat hypothetical nomenclature and made a rigorous attempt to establish a critical context for a group of American avant-garde films. What I discovered was a rich system of resemblance between the form and content of these films and the techniques and themes of the Decadent/Symbolist movement which had been inspired by the French poet Charles Baudelaire.

The films selected for a Baudelairean Cinema filmography were chosen for their Decadent and Symbolist concerns. Naturally, the prototype of the Baudelairean Cinema is *Flaming Creatures*. Although Jonas Mekas states that one of Jacobs/Fleischner's earlier works, *Blonde Cobra*, is the seminal film, it is *Flaming Creatures'* notoriety and its history of negative social response which place it as titular head of a Baudelairean filmography.

To place Baudelairean films in a historical and critical context within the avant-garde cinema, I have used a method based on a system of juxtapositions in which one poetic medium illuminates another. I selected certain characteristics of French Decadence and Symbolism from the works of artists of the late nineteenth century to make points of comparison between those works and the work of the Baudelairean Cinema of the 1960s. It was my hope that such a comparison would illuminate themes, imagery, and aesthetics common to both eras.

1

What is the Baudelairean Cinema?

The American Underground Film

If we ask the question, "What is the Baudelairean Cinema?" we must begin by answering the question, "Who is Jonas Mekas?" It was Mekas (a New York film critic) who coined the term "Baudelairean Cinema,"[1] and the fact that it was Mekas is significant. No artist within the American avant-garde film has equaled Jonas Mekas's influence as a polemicist; his influence as a critic was at its height in 1963 when he proclaimed the birth of the "Baudelairean Cinema".

Mekas and his brother Adolfas had founded *Film Culture*[2] (the only regularly published journal which became almost entirely devoted to American avant-garde film) in 1955, five years after coming to the United States from Lithuania by way of postwar Germany. Although at first the Mekas's editorial position was strongly opposed to experimental film, in 1959 the essay "A Call for a New Generation of Film-makers" indicated the transition from that position to another (from international low budget commercial productions of high artistic interest to independently made American experimental films: "The New American Cinema"[3]). The magazine became the house organ for the rising Underground cinema in the United States throughout the 1960s. The nineteenth issue, published in 1959, established the Independent Film Award to mark "the entrance of a new generation of filmmakers into American cinema."[4] The Award editorial also proclaimed the death of Hollywood. Over the following years, *Film Culture's* Independent Film Award was won by Stan Brakhage, Jack Smith, Andy Warhol, and Kenneth Anger, among others.

In 1960, Mekas organized a series of special screenings at the Charles Street Theatre on New York's Lower East Side. These were one-man shows for avant-garde filmmakers whose work had never been completely shown in New York. Mekas was also the instigating force in the formation of the New York Film-makers' Cooperative, a distribution center for independently produced films. The Cooperative became the first open distribution structure for personal, noncommercial films. This was a major breakthrough in independent distribution: before it began in 1961, few personal and independently made films had any chance of national distribution. By 1968, there were approximately 150 commercial and noncommercial theatres regularly showing avant-garde works. These films were labeled variously during the sixties as "The New American Cinema," "Experimental," "Independent," or "Underground" film.[5]

Mekas also organized the Film-makers' Cinémathèque, the Friends of the New Cinema (a foundation which gave small grants to approximately 12 filmmakers each year between 1964 and 1971), and Anthology Film Archives.[6] He was best known to readers for his column "Movie Journal" in *The Village Voice* (1958–75) and for his extensive writings for *Film Culture*, which he edited and published.

In addition to becoming the champion of "The New American Cinema" and one of its most influential critics in America, Mekas worked alone and with his brother as an independent filmmaker. Most of the Mekas's films are personal newsreels (documentary material, subjectively manipulated by technique). The brothers' shift in interest from international feature productions to American experimental films was partially due to the difficulties they had encountered in getting financing and distribution for their own films.

The increase in accessibility, distribution and viewing, as well as the constant critical attention paid to them by Mekas in the *Voice*, were responsible for the emergence of certain independent filmmakers and trends in the American avant-garde cinema. Before examining the trend under study here—the Baudelairean Cinema—it might be useful to review certain characteristics prevalent in American avant-garde or experimental cinema in the 1960s.

1.   Avant-garde cinema is usually produced outside the commercial film framework. And, since these are not commercial films made primarily to entertain, the spectator does not expect certain formulas or conventions of style and plot. Instead of intending to relax an audience, the avant-garde film is often made to jolt the viewer out of his/her complacency. Therefore these films have no need to appeal to a large audience to earn back million-dollar production expenses.

2.   These films are generally conceived and executed by a single individual. By definition, most avant-garde films are *auteurist*, i.e., they are often shot, edited, processed, printed (sometimes cooked or destroyed) and projected by one artist who makes all the major artistic decisions.

3.   This autonomy has freed the filmmaker to turn to his/her own life, and avant-garde films contain many autobiographical elements. The filmmaker may also create biographies and turn to friends and other artists as

subject matter. For example, among Andy Warhol's early film efforts are portraits of his artist friends Robert Indiana (in *Eat*) and John Giorno (in *Sleep*).

4.   Given their limited distribution, avant-garde films usually are not subjected to censorship and they often treat taboo subjects in an outrageous and shocking manner. Many would, in fact, probably be judged immoral by an audience accustomed to commercial film. To be shocking and outrageous was, as we shall see, an aesthetic impulse which developed throughout the 1960s, particularly in the Underground Film classification, in which films were not only unconventional but deliberately anticonventional in their use of form and content.

5.   Technically, avant-garde films, from France in the 1920s to New York in the 1970s, have always been a seedbed of innovation. Possibilities of trick photography were examined as early as the turn of the century by Méliès, and again in France in the 1920s by surrealists such as Man Ray and Marcel Duchamp. Trick (special effects) techniques were further developed in America in the 1940s and used to explore the possibilities for subjective expression.

6.   Probably the most consistently important distinguishing characteristic of the avant-garde cinema has been its experimentation with nonlinear time and nondiegetic screen-space. Most avant-garde films experiment with new forms of time and space in cinema. Some are even against the time-space continuum in much the same way the surrealists were against these conventions in literary and dramatic narrative. Narratives are traditional forms in literature and drama; the avant-garde operates outside established traditions and seeks to invent new forms.

The characteristics of avant-garde film in general are visible in that portion of the American avant-garde called the Underground Film. The term Underground Film became a journalistic commonplace after 1962. It was first used by critic Manny Farber in 1957 to describe a type of masculine adventure film of the 1930s and 1940s.[7] Much later the term appeared in an entirely different context in an article in the winter issue of *Film Quarterly* in 1961.[8] In it, Stan VanDerBeek used the term "Underground" to describe the period of filmmaking in America which began in the late 1950s and flourished in the mid-1960s. In this category he included his own films, Jack Smith's *Flaming Creatures*, and the earliest films of Andy Warhol.

The question, "What is Underground Film?" is best answered by Sheldon Renan in *An Introduction to the American Underground Film* (1967).[9] Beginning with the second half of the 1950s in America, the terms "Independent" and "Underground" arose. "Independent," according to Renan, signified films made by filmmakers free of the Hollywood structure.[10] Underground Film differed from Independent in that it was comprised largely of noncommercial films. Economically restricted by their non-commercial status, Underground filmmakers generally worked in 16mm (an advantage in terms of the greater availability of projection facilities). The films had to be cheap, so they were necessarily shorter in length than features; most Underground films were under thirty minutes in running time. (There are obvious exceptions to these compromises, such as Stan Brakhage's *Songs* in 8mm, and Warhol's eight-hour portrait of the Empire State Building.)

At the Fourth Experimental Film Festival in Knokke-le-Zoute, Belgium in 1967-68, a conference between representatives of European and American avant-garde film cooperatives stressed that "the word 'Underground' should be avoided because to some of the public it meant dirty movies, to others, amateur films."[11] But the Underground label continued to enjoy wide usage throughout the 1960s because exhibitors could draw larger audiences with this more evocative word than with the other terms then in use (such as "Experimental" or "New American Cinema").

The subject matter in Underground Film was usually "documentary," but this material, often taken from the filmmaker's actual environment, was fictionalized in the process of filming and editing. For the Underground filmmaker, actual life was seen as "the raw material to be manipulated into the form of [the filmmaker's] personal perspective."[12] A fictionalization of biographical and autobiographical material was generally an avant-garde characteristic and the manipulation of such subject matter in the Underground Film was successfully extended to include portraiture. For example, in 1963, Andy Warhol had started to make close-up portraits: *Kiss*, primarily a series of close-ups of the filmmaker Naomi Levine kissing various companions; *Sleep*, a six-hour portrait of a man (poet John Giorno) sleeping; *Haircut*, thirty minutes of a man having his hair cut; *Eat*, forty-five minutes of painter Robert Indiana eating a mushroom; and his most famous portrait, *Henry Geldzahler*: one-hundred minutes of the artist-entrepreneur smoking a cigar.[13] Jonas Mekas wrote of these portraits in his "Movie Journal" column in *The Village Voice*, "I think that Andy Warhol is the most revolutionary of all filmmakers working today."[14]

Biographical portraiture in the Underground Film was responsible for the advent of what Mekas called the "Emergence of the Underground Star Cinema,"[15] in the American avant-garde of the 1960s. For example, *Pull My Daisy* (1959), often considered the first Underground Film, "starred" the most notable of the Beat poets—Allen Ginsberg, Gregory Corso, and Peter Orlovsky, and "it retains the feeling of a freely improvised film. . . . It was based on a scene from an unproduced play by Jack Kerouac,[16] who speaks for all the characters on the soundtrack, adding comments of his own."[17] *Pull My Daisy* was created within a fictional framework but filmed as documentary reality, a technique typical of the Underground Film. It was a home-movie in that it was made by and about a group of friends—the look of informality, intimate portrayals of people at play, "clownin' around," is strongly evinced in the early films of Jack Smith and Ken Jacobs (*Little Stabs of Happiness*, 1958; *Scotchtape*, 1962). Ron Rice's *The Flower Thief* (1960) used Beat clown Taylor Mead's "humorous hi-jinks" in much the same manner. This continued use of artists-at-play as Underground Film motif encouraged the development of an acting style of "calculated madness."[18] This style reached its zenith in Jack Smith's *Flaming Creatures* (1963), the Underground Film classic in which almost all of the action takes place during an orgy—indeed here, as elsewhere (*Chumlum, Inauguration of the Pleasure Dome*), the orgy serves as theatrical device. Almost all the Underground Films which became a part of the Baudelairean Cinema trend were engrossed with "performers" and "performances"—two concerns which avant-garde cinema had *not* stressed prior to the films of Ron Rice, Jack Smith, Andy Warhol, et al. In the 1960s home-movie portraiture became a stylistic commonplace in American Underground Film.

Although Underground Film was distinguished by its style and technique, its unique contribution within the avant-garde tradition was the emphasis Underground filmmakers placed on film-acting. A careful attention to "performance" in Underground cinema was due to three factors. First, the long-take, immobile camera technique used in Andy Warhol's early films, in which the camera was chiefly a "recording" device, liberated the interpretation of the subject matter, leaving the bulk of the interpretation to the subject him/herself. Secondly, the 1960s were rich in theatrical innovations and improvisational groups: of the latter, the most well-known were the Living Theatre and the Theatre of the Ridiculous. During the mid-1960s many of the impromptu and highly improbable scripts written for the Theatre of the Ridiculous were developed into film scripts for an important phase of Andy Warhol's filmmaking career.[19] The theatrical performers were in many cases the same actors who had appeared earlier in the films of Jack Smith and Ken Jacobs. The third factor responsible for the emergence of Underground Film "stars" was the emphasis which Mekas placed on the actor (Underground "stars") in his writing. Comparing Underground actors to Hollywood stars, he even described Taylor Mead's performance in *The Queen of Sheba Meets the Atom Man* (Ron Rice, 1963) as comparable to the best work of Chaplin, Keaton, or Langdon and "a portrayal capable of establishing him as one of the screen's greatest performers."[20]

Jonas Mekas (as well as Adolfas) had studied with Ippolitas Tvirbutas,[21] a teacher of the Stanislavsky method of acting, and it was evidently Mekas's great interest in the method and its goals—transformation from mere acting into performance, or the breaking down of the difference between the performer and his role—which inspired him to write in his "Notes on The New American Cinema," "Improvisation is the highest form of condensation, it points to the very essence of a thought, an emotion, a movement."[22]

In a critique of *Flaming Creatures*, Susan Sontag analyzed the film's technical qualities by expanding the concepts of informality, intimacy, and "calculated madness" of prior Underground Films. In describing *Flaming Creatures* as an Underground Film, Sontag wrote in 1964:

> The hallmark of one of the two new avant-garde styles in American cinema (Jack Smith, Ron Rice, *et al.*, but not Gregory Markopoulos or Stan Brakhage) is its willful technical crudity. The new films—both the good ones and the poor, uninspired work—show a maddening indifference to every element of technique, a studied primitiveness. This is a very contemporary style, and very American.[23]

Sontag counts seven "clearly" separate sequences within the film, but no "story" is evident.

> Of no sequence is one convinced that it had to last this long, and not longer or shorter. Shots aren't framed in the traditional way; heads are cut off; extraneous figures sometimes appear on the margin of the scene. The camera is hand-held most of the time, and the image often quivers . . .[24]

Mekas, in his *Voice* columns, pointed out the techniques of the Underground that had become technical clichés by the mid-1960s: "hand-held camera, out-of-focus shots, shaky camera technique, improvised acting, single frames, jumpy cutting,"[25] and direct manipulation of filmic material, for example, by painting on or scratching film. Underground films looked technically amateurish on purpose. Some of the "scabrous vitality" of such films as *Blonde Cobra* or *Flaming Creatures* came from their crude technique and "lack of technical finish."[26] Jonas Mekas saw these "out-of-focus shots, the shaky shots, the unsure steps, the hesitant movements, the over-exposed and under-exposed bits" as "part of the new cinema vocabulary, being part of the psychological and visual reality of modern man."[27]

In this chapter we have seen how the Underground Film movement departed from certain earlier avant-garde film characteristics. Utilizing a style of technical crudity, it moved toward a more personalized, informal mode: it adapted an improvisational-theatre approach; in developing as an extension of a radical theatre group it became a "radicalized" form of avant-garde or experimental film. This was predictable since Underground Film developed within the avant-garde cinema during the 1960s, a time when there was an explosion of personal art filmmaking. Out of this explosion, Mekas discovered and "named" a new type of cinema, a subcategory of the Underground Film. His designation—the Baudelairean Cinema—was the first "naming" of a trend within Underground Film.

Form and Structure of the Baudelairean Cinema

If we looked for one single myth common to all of Baudelairean Cinema, we should have difficulty in finding a suitable choice. Our major problem, in fact, might be selecting one from many. Variations of myths of death and rebirth are practically conventions in the Underground Film and these myths occur even more abundantly in the Baudelairean Cinema. Myths of the Apocalypse offer another possibility. Decadence has been defined as more than a perverse expression of pre-apocalyptic dissatisfaction: it includes the Apocalypse proper—the celebration which signals the new age. In his genre study of the Western, *Horizons West* (1969), Jim Kitses reminds us that "myth has to do with the activity of gods,"[28] and in Baudelairean Cinema, we consistently find the classic Greek and Biblical myths which reflect cyclic themes of death and rebirth. The myth of Persephone is the elemental material of *Flaming Creatures*; the Phoenix born from the ashes is basic to Kenneth Anger's *Fireworks*.

The Baudelairean Cinema is eclectic: many myths donate subject matter; no one myth is required to "tell" the story; and myth is used for its symbolic material. Situations and characters are lifted from other myths and combined in the Baudelairean Cinema to convey such oppositions as loss of energy/renewal of energy; self-destruction/purification; decadence/spirituality. For example, the Biblical myths of Salomé, Judith and Holphernes, and Lilith all contain themes of redemption through sin. In each, the strong woman destroys the weak male, a familiar decadent conceit examined later in this paper.

In the literature of the French Decadent writers, Christian myths of resurrection and redemption abound; these reappear among the Baudelairean filmmakers. The French Decadents themselves often used Decadence as a concept for "redemption through sin": a ritual of purification. Joris-Karl Huysmans, Charles Baudelaire, and Paul Verlaine all ultimately fled from their self-proclaimed orgies of self-destruction. After reaching disillusionment by way of debauchery, they reembraced the Catholic Church. Huysmans, who could be considered the chief penitent of the three, wrote at the end of his introduction to *A rebours* (*Against the Grain*) (1884) that for him there remained only the choice between the bullet or the cross.[29]

But whether salvation was achieved through self-destruction or a last-minute clutch at the rosary, the Decadent writers moved through extremes of sensuality toward a new spirituality. The Decadent/Symbolist aesthetic was based on more than Christian or pagan myths; the most important emphasis was on the loss and rediscovery of energy (psychic as well as physical). A concern with élan vital is a theme which we can trace in all of the films of the Baudelairean Cinema, a trend which leads to the inevitable reoccurrence of certain themes. The themes, in this case, happen to be identical with the themes of an already established literary form: the Decadent novel of fin de siècle France.

The Baudelairean Cinema emphasizes themes of demonic possession as expressed through the loss and recovery of psychic and physical power. Aspects of demonic possession appear in several titles: *Flaming Creatures, Fireworks, Invocation to My Demon Brother, Scorpio Rising,* and *Lucifer Rising.* The theme is played out by the main characters in almost every film. Demonic possession is expressed through the powerful characters from Anger's mythology; characterizations of "real" vampires appear in Smith's films. Moreover, several of Warhol's "superstars" suggest the extremes of personal power, a power implied by their screen names—Ultra Violet, Ingrid Superstar, Pope Ondine, and Viva—as well as their screen personalities.

Through the repetition of recurring motifs, Baudelairean films convey a vision, if not always a story, and the themes invariably reflect several different myths which transcend time and space. In Baudelairean Cinema, themes from myths are visualized and illuminated instead of told.

At this point, we must ask: what are the techniques and forms in Baudelairean film which make up a nonlinear structure? How do the films transcend temporal/spatial continuity? Narrative in Baudelairean film is accomplished by a form of synaesthesia which operates in basic Symbolist tradition: bonds of correspondence between elements within the film form clear symbolic relationships which refer to a metasystem outside or beyond their system. This system of correspondences is best illustrated by Anger's *Scorpio Rising*, in which there is a symbolic relationship between music and lyrics, and the image and color. Through the interaction of correspondences, several themes are emphasized and many myths are combined.

In films such as *Flaming Creatures* or *Blonde Cobra*, as well as in many of Warhol's films, there is no importance placed on the passage of time, and the actions take place in claustrophobic, abstract sets: struggles between characters are repeated in sequences resembling vaudeville skits (the most formal) or happenings (the least formal). Here the struggles and repetitions are no more than loose patterns of action differentiated by rambling narration or vocal noises interspersed with scratchy old records from the 1930s and 1940s. Throughout *Flaming Creatures*, one scratched record follows another, accompanied by screams, commentary and electronic ringing, all of which creates a synaesthetic relationship between words, music, and visual movement. The separation of sensual bombardment is minimally sufficient to divide the film into movements, or, as Susan Sontag suggests, "sequences": "There is, of course, no story in *Flaming Creatures*, no development, no necessary order of the seven (as I count them) clearly separable sequences of the film."[30] Of no sequence is one convinced that any pattern of action is finite.

Smith's film is strictly a treat for the senses. There is no geographical "setting." Smith uses no recognizable background. Instead, the characters themselves form a visual landscape which foregrounds any literal idea of *place*. This foregrounding material is composed of movements (camera and character), camera framing (often empty or partially filled), and shots of forced perspective (extreme close-ups without visual reference shots). This thoroughly artificial and invented landscape is played out against a background of banal songs, advertisements, clothes, dances, and, above all, the repertory of fantasy drawn from corny Hollywood movies. The texture of *Flaming Creatures* is made up of a rich collage of camp lore. Sontag wrote:

> The space in which *Flaming Creatures* moves is not the space of moral ideas, which is where American critics have traditionally located art. What I am urging is that there is not only moral space, by whose laws *Flaming Creatures* would have come off badly; there is also aesthetic space, the space of pleasure. Here Smith's film moves and has its being.[31]

We have seen how spatial continuity is transcended in *Flaming Creatures* by sensuality and a sort of collage form (analyzed in chapter 5 of this book). In Kenneth Anger's films temporal/spatial continuity is replaced with a highly sophisticated and refined system of correspondences. In his *Eaux d'Artifice, Puce Moment, KKK,* and *Scorpio Rising,* structural synaesthesia is achieved by his orchestration of sound and color which play on the spectator's senses, an orchestration which emphasizes themes inherent in the film. For instance in the "Blue Velvet" sequence in *Scorpio* pop lyrics describing a dress of blue velvet, in contrast to visuals of the male protagonist who is wearing blue denim levis. The romantic "she" wearing velvet is quite obviously a he (see chapter 5). Often in Baudelairean films, popular songs provide the only sound on the films' soundtrack.

Anger and Smith take different advantage of the nostalgic resonances of pop music; Anger places a film in a specific "AM radio-time". This is the time zone in which a song got the most airplay on popular radio and, therefore, becomes the time when the film is forever taking place. Anger's images serve as a social documentary of the era. The pop narrative lyrics serve, simultaneously, as a social commentary on the images.

Jack Smith, on the other hand, created *Flaming Creatures* to look "out-of-date" from its inception. He used outdated army film stock and shot the film atop the oldest surviving theatre in New York City; he dressed his creatures in superannuated finery. Smith's film gives one the feeling that it might simply be a record of nightly cavortings in a graveyard. The film looks backward toward a time which never really existed or, which exists without end, as Smith experienced it in the films of his beloved Maria Montez.

Smith's use of dated music reinforces the ancient, rotting qualities of his images. The music is "used," familiar music, lifted from the soundtracks of old films. It has the same ambience as the "stock shot" in conventional filmmaking. Sometimes it has the easy recognizability of George Gershwin's "Let's Call the Whole Thing Off," sung by Fred Astaire at the opening of *Blonde Cobra*. When Smith sets his creatures dreamily dancing to 1930s tango music in *Flaming Creatures*, it becomes an invocation of old Hollywood, an attempt to make lost glamour reappear by creating imitations of the past (especially as typified by the South Sea Island epics of Maria Montez and Jon Hall). The most striking invocation to a lost Hollywood era is Mario Montez's sultry fandango to "Siboney," reminiscent of the Latin America musicals of the 1930s of which *Flying Down to Rio* (1933) was the prototype.

However, it is, finally, a style of "Camp" which can be used to isolate the Baudelairean filmmaker. In her definitive essay on the nature of "Camp," Susan Sontag lists well over fifty Camp sensibilities and characteristics. Let us cite a few of these descriptions and mention those Baudelairean filmmakers whose techniques most strongly reflect them:

A. Camp is a certain mode of aestheticism.

   ... Camp sensibility is disengaged, depoliticized—or at least apolitical.[32]
   [Warhol / Smith / Rice]

B. ... Camp art is often decorative art, emphasizing texture, sensuous surface, and style at the expense of content.[33]
   [Smith / Rice]

C. All Camp objects, and persons, contain a large element of artifice. Nothing in nature can be campy ...[34]
   [Smith / Warhol. Anger transcends this Camp characteristic with his highly idealized use of natural landscape in such films as *Eaux d'Artifice* and *Lucifer Rising*.]

D. ... love of the exaggerated.

   The androgyne is certainly one of the great images of Camp sensibility. ... the haunting androgynous vacancy behind the perfect beauty of Greta Garbo.[35]
   [Smith / Rice]

E. ... a relish for the exaggeration of sexual characteristics and personality mannerisms ... the corny flamboyant femaleness of Jayne Mansfield ... the exaggerated he-manness of Steve Reeves, Victor Mature.[36]
   [Warhol / Smith, and, to a lesser extent, Anger.]

F. To camp is a mode of seduction—one which employs flamboyant mannerisms susceptible of a double interpretation; gestures full of duplicity ...[37]
   [Warhol / Smith / Anger / Rice]

Sontag goes on to write:

... in the 19th century, what had been distributed throughout all of high culture now becomes a special taste; it takes on overtones of the acute, the esoteric, the perverse. Confining the story to England alone, we see Camp continuing wanly through 19th

century aestheticism (Burne-Jones, Pater, Ruskin, Tennyson), emerging full-blown with
the Art Nouveau movement in the visual and decorative arts, and finding its conscious
ideologists in such "wits" as Wilde and Firbank.[38]

Here Sontag is writing of the nineteenth-century aestheticism which flourished in France as the Mauve Decade. The parallels between Sontag's
definition of Camp and the aesthetics of the nineteenth-century French
Decadents support our comparison between the 1890s and the 1960s.

It seems evident after examining the technique and content of Baudelairean Cinema that these films constitute a trend which is, in its own way, as
distinct as the work of the nineteenth-century Decadent/Symbolist artists.

To understand more deeply those films which Mekas describes as
examples of the Baudelairean Cinema, we must take seriously his references
to de Sade and the nineteenth-century poets (see Mekas's article in Appendix
A). Indeed it is their world of "flowers of evil" which Mekas sees blooming
afresh in the films of this trend.

Unfortunately, Mekas was correct in predicting the public outrage these
films were to be met with. They, like Charles Baudelaire's *Les Fleurs du mal*
(*The Flowers of Evil*),[39] were heavily censored and rejected for their
"decadence." The majority of the films remained inaccessible because of
production and distribution problems extant in the "Underground" conditions of the American experimental film in the 1960s. Unfortunately, the
films did not survive these conditions with much success and they remain
relatively nonviewable to the larger, more sophisticated avant-garde film
audiences of today. Like those films which Mekas names, the poetry of
Baudelaire was also "too 'decadent' for the 'average' man in any organized
culture;" his works were reviled and banned for their perversity. Baudelaire's
complete works did not become publicly available until after his death. The
author was placed on trial for obscenity immediately following the first
edition of *Fleurs* in 1857.

The film *Flaming Creatures* was also persecuted and banned; in 1967
David Curtis wrote about the film's "subversive content":

. . . our enthusiasm was expressed almost entirely in terms of *Flaming Creatures'*
subversive content, the degree to which it defied the accepted aesthetic and moral codes of
cinema. It was acclaimed as evidence of one man's cerebral and sexual emancipation.[40]

The sexual "subversion" of a film like *Flaming Creatures* made it almost
impossible to screen: the film had its New York premiere at the Grammercy
Arts Theatre in February of 1964. It was first seized by the New York Police
in March of that same year, and was seized a second time by detectives from
the District Attorney's Office of New York on May 12, 1964.[41] In his "Movie
Journal" column Mekas wrote that on June 18, 1964, *Flaming Creatures* was

declared obscene by the New York Criminal Court (about the same time as Kenneth Anger's *Scorpio Rising* was banned in Los Angeles).[42] Four years later, the film still could not be legally screened:

> [In the autumn of] 1968 a print of Jack Smith's film *Flaming Creatures* was seized at the University of Michigan. The case is still open. Meanwhile enemies of [Supreme Court] Justice [Abe] Fortas, manipulators of justice, got a print of Jack's film from Detroit police, and are circulating it in Washington, D.C., among the Senators, to undermine Fortas.[43]

Obviously it would be somewhat superficial to unite the works of Jack Smith (and others) with those of Baudelaire solely on the basis of censorship. To discover exactly what is "Baudelairean" about such films as *Blonde Cobra* and *Flaming Creatures* it is necessary for us to take Mekas's suggestion quite literally and to return to the aesthetics of nineteenth-century France in order to examine the concepts which comprised the world view of Charles Baudelaire and others. For the purpose of this study, we shall find it necessary to expand our concept of "Baudelairean" to include the development of this world view as it was expressed within the literature and art of the fin de siècle. We shall then be able to examine the Baudelairean Cinema through its relationship to the aesthetics of French Decadence/Symbolism.

2

Baudelaire and the Decadent/Symbolist Movement in France

Introduction

Although analogy is not a method for establishing identity, and it does not adequately define a set of films in the sense of isolating identifying characteristics, nevertheless, it will be used here as a first step toward establishing a method for study. Analogy will be later used to suggest parallels between the art and literature of the nineteenth century in France and the films of the American Baudelairean Cinema of the 1960s. We shall use analogy, in short, to select a set of American Underground films which are reflective of a Baudelairean sensibility (one which combines the aesthetics of Baudelaire with those of the French Decadence).

Some Motifs in Baudelaire

The Crowd Motif

When studying Baudelaire it is useful both to relate him to and separate him from the Romantic movement. Just as Romantic artists had relied on the verdant chaos of nature to provide them with material, Baudelaire turned to the richness of urban life for his poetic imagery. As John Middleton Murry has pointed out, Baudelaire's France was in an "age of rampant industrialism and violent and abortive revolution; of the hideous and uncontrolled eruption of the great cities; of all the squalor of a victorious and hypocritical materialism."[1] As we shall see, Baudelaire expressed the decadence of the era of "progress, that great heresy of decay . . . "[2]

Baudelaire has been called "the great poet of the modern city,"[3] and Walter Benjamin pointed out that the poet thought of himself as a "man of the crowd."[4] As Baudelaire described it in his essay "Le Peintre de la vie moderne" ("The Painter of Modern Life"),

... the lover of universal life moves into the crowd as though into an enormous reservoir of electricity. He, the lover of life, may also be compared to a mirror as vast as this crowd; to a kaleidoscope endowed with consciousness, which with every one of its movements presents a pattern of life, in all its multiplicity, and the flowing grace of all the elements that go to compose life.[5]

He relied on the "Muse of modern time"[6] and his own immersion in the multitudes of Paris for stimulation and inspiration. Benjamin believed that for Baudelaire the masses were an agitated veil, and through it Baudelaire saw Paris:

... he let the spectacle of the crowd act upon him. The deepest fascination of this spectacle lay in the fact that as it intoxicated him it did not blind him to the horrible social reality. He remained conscious of it, though only in the way in which intoxicated are "still" aware of reality. That is why in Baudelaire the big city almost never finds expression in the direct presentation of its inhabitants.[7]

The crowd motif in Baudelaire's work is one of the aspects which separate him from Romanticism; the Romantic poets placed emphasis on the isolated hero, the noble savage, the individual in nature. In Baudelaire's poetry, the crowd is reflected in the movement, rhythm, and imagery. Benjamin described *Les Fleurs du mal* as a form of literature which relied on the power to shock: "Baudelaire placed the shock experience at the very centre of his artistic work."[8] The manner in which certain of Baudelaire's images shock the reader can be likened to that experienced by a pedestrian in a crowd of people. The violation of the senses in his poetry is similar to that which one endures when being jostled about, making tactile and visual contact with the metropolitan masses. As Baudelaire wrote, "What perils have the forest and the prairie to compare with the daily shocks and conflicts of civilization?"[9]

L'art pour l'art

Despite the stimulation of urban life which provided Baudelaire with much of his poetic imagery, one of his strongest theoretical convictions was the Decadent/Symbolist doctrine of *l'art pour l'art*. This theory began to become fashionable in Parisian literary circles after the publication of Théophile Gautier's *Mademoiselle de Maupin* (1835). The novel *Maupin* was a harbinger of French Decadence and its themes, as it dictated that art had no utilitarian value—either social, political, or religious; art existed in its own right, was its own *raison d'être*, and was independent of any didactic function. Gautier, in his Preface to *Mademoiselle de Maupin*, wrote: "I would rather give up potatoes than roses . . . . Everything useful is ugly for it is the expression of some need."[10] Baudelaire, who dedicated *Fleurs* to

Gautier, wrote of *Maupin*: " . . . this hymn to Beauty, so to speak, had above all the important result of establishing once and for all the exclusive love of the Beautiful, the *Fixed Idea* as the generating condition of works of art."[11]

Artificiality

In 1851 Baudelaire had declared that art could not be separated from utility, but almost immediately recanted this position and actively espoused *l'art pour l'art* until he died in 1867. In Preface II to *Fleurs* he described the book as "quintessentially useless and absolutely innocent . . . . "[12] His desire for perfection of form over content also explains his championing the cause: "Nature is ugly, and I prefer the monsters of my imagination to the triteness of actuality."[13] This statement also reflects Baudelaire's love of artificiality, a belief in the superiority of artifice over nature, a view which is more Decadent than Romantic. It is easy to see how this motif of artificiality in both his poetry and prose was related to his belief in art for art's sake. This cult of artificiality was to continue to evolve as an important motif in Decadent aesthetics.

In addition to the two important motifs of the crowd and the doctrine of art for art's sake, we must consider several other themes in Baudelaire's work. He was very much preoccupied with death and Satanism, as well as with the characters of the dandy, the vampire, and the lesbian. These subjects were all deeply rooted in French Romanticism and later became major contributions to the Decadent world view. They are essential themes found in *Fleurs*, and they can most obviously be found in the works of Edgar Allan Poe and the Marquis de Sade, two major influences on Baudelaire: " . . . the Baudelaire of his own age was the satanic Baudelaire, who gathered into a choice bouquet the strangest orchids, the most monstrous aroids from among the wild tropical flora of French Romanticism."[14]

Death

When the second, revised edition of *Fleurs* came out in 186¹ in Belgium, a group of six poems (out of thirty-five new pieces) under the heading "La Mort" ("Death") had been added to the original (which had been published and prosecuted for obscenity in 1857). A dominating theme in almost all the poems in *Fleurs* was that of death. For Baudelaire desire was immutably linked with death, as in "You Whom I Worship":

> I leap to your attack, climb in assault,
> Like corpseworms feeding nimbly in the vault,
> And cherish you, relentless, cruel beast,
> Till that last coolness which delights me best.[15]

The theme of death, in which "love is a stain which obstinately lingers,"[16] is clearly Romantic in origin (as has been demonstrated by Mario Praz in his study *The Romantic Agony*).

Satanism

In *Fleurs*, Baudelaire had attempted to, in his own words, "extract *beauty* from Evil."[17] For him, the very nature of Beauty was at stake. His theory can be more closely linked with that of the Marquis de Sade, who held that it was evil that was man's prime motivation toward pleasure. And, as Marcel Ruff has pointed out:

> The distance between pleasure and aesthetic excitement is not great, especially if one accepts Stendhal's statement that: "Beauty is but the promise of happiness." Baudelaire certainly did not intend to make the artist one of Satan's henchmen, or Beauty the exclusive product of Hell. But he was not content with illusions on this subject. Human nature being what it is, art, like any other activity of man, necessarily feeds on Evil, just as much as on Good.[18]

The Dandy

Baudelaire first wrote of the dandy in a section of his essay on painter Constantin Guys's "Le Peintre de la vie moderne," entitled simply "Le Dandy."[19] There were later fleeting references in his posthumously published *Journaux intimes* (*Intimate Journals*), and, as Marcel Ruff has stated: "The importance he attached to it can be perceived from the article he was planning to write on the subject from 1860 until the last moments of his literary activity."[20] The article was to have been entitled, "Le Dandysme littéraire, ou la Grandeur sans convictions" ("Literary Dandyism, or Grandeur without Convictions").[21]

For Baudelaire, dandyism was a passion; what he called:

> . . . the burning desire to create a personal form of originality, within the external limits of social conventions . . . . It is the pleasure of causing surprise in others, and the proud satisfaction of never showing any oneself.[22]

We can find a key to Baudelaire's stance in his proclamation that whatever dandies may call themselves:

> . . . all share the same characteristic of opposition and revolt; all are representatives of what is best in human pride, of that need, which is too rare in the modern generation, to combat and destroy triviality. That is the source, in your dandy, of that haughty, patrician attitude, aggressive even in its coldness.[23]

It has already been pointed out that Baudelaire lived in a period of uncontrolled "progress"; a progress which had promoted in the great majority of the "modern generation" a devotion to a way of life based only on material needs, desires and interests. In that trend Baudelaire saw a denial of the spiritual in man, a denial of the only possible progress he believed that man could make—moral progress. He concluded that:

> . . . if this deplorable madness continues for long, the decadent races will fall into the drivelling sleep of decrepitude on the pillow of destiny. This infatuation is the symptom of a decadence that is already too obvious.[24]

Baudelaire thus became a dandy to protect himself from the corrupting influences of materialism which, in his eyes, manifested itself so perversely. He absented himself from this world, believing that, in the affected actions and outlook of a dandy, he would be more capable of functioning in the modern decadent world. He became the victor instead of the victim. Baudelaire believed that "Dandyism is the last flicker of heroism in decadent ages . . . "[25] Looking for a model on which to base his dandy, he wrote in his *Journaux intimes*:

> I have found a definition of the Beautiful, of my own conception of the Beautiful. It is something intense and sad . . . .
> I can scarcely conceive . . . a type of Beauty which has nothing to do with Sorrow. In pursuit of—others might say obsessed by—these ideas, it may be supposed that I have difficulty in not concluding from them that the most perfect type of manly beauty is Satan—as Milton saw him.[26]

Mario Praz in his analysis of Milton's conception of Satan cited E.W. Tillyard's statement ". . . the character of Satan expresses as no other character or act or feature of the poem [*Paradise Lost*] does, something in which Milton believed very strongly: heroic energy."[27]

Clearly, we can see an element of narcissism in Baudelaire's dandy. As he declared: "The Dandy should aspire to be uninterruptedly sublime. He should live and sleep in front of a mirror."[28] The dandy conceived of himself as a work of art; a work tempered by the conditions of modern civilization. Dandies had no other function, said Baudelaire, but that of "cultivating the idea of beauty in their own persons, of satisfying their passions, of feeling and thinking."[29] He also called the dandy: ". . . the . . . supreme incarnation of the idea of the beautiful given expression in material life, he who dictates form and governs manners," and ". . . proof of an inventive faculty which for a long time has deserted us."[30]

Repulsed, and yet perversely attracted to the life that he knew in Paris,

Baudelaire conceived of the dandy as proof of his victory over its decadent conditions. He believed in the "eternal superiority of the Dandy."[31]

It might be said of the dandy that he was Romantic internally and Decadent externally; his manner of life required severe discipline and unimpassioned self-sacrifice to Romantic goals, which, by their very nature remained ideal and unfulfilled. There was an intellectual Romanticism represented in the ideal of the dandy. Baudelaire himself pointed out:

> "Le Dandy" is an imperturbable being above the law, inscrutable, contemptuous of the world, silent under the torments which it inflects upon his sensitive soul, continually experimenting at his own risk with morality, exercising a drastic discipline upon himself, and adopting, as a symbol of his inward discipline, that elegance of outward appearance which we generally associate with the word "dandy".[32]

The aesthetics and moral isolation of the dandy is a concept directly related to *l'art pour l'art*. His narcissism and self-consciousness render him inaccessible and therefore *consciously* useless to modern society.

The Vampire

Baudelaire, in the manner of a true dandy, objectified the heroine in his love poems, worshipping her from a distance, creating and cursing her all in one breath. This Romantic idealization of the unknowable love object is one method the poet uses to distance himself from his subject matter; the object of desire can never be realized, possessed, captured, or framed. The obsession to possess is constantly frustrated by the poet's desire to "know" her, to analyze his beloved ideal from a privileged distance.

The subjects of his love poems in *Fleurs* are Jeanne Duval/Lemer or La Présidente.[33] In both instances the woman is a mute idol; she is seen in Baudelaire's eyes as "the object on the magician's baton . . . . "[34] Again, artifice is preferable to nature, or "in other words, as to the woman herself, the poet prefers the image of her which he makes or unmakes at will."[35] Throughout these poems, the heroine is seen, in turn, as a monster, a mistress, or death; the closest the poet comes to realizing a form of Romantic love is a sort of ecstatic vampirism. In "Le Vampire" (1855) and "Le Léthé" (1857), among others in the "Spleen et Ideal" ("Bile and the Ideal") section of *Fleurs*, the poet is obsessed with an impossible love. This obsession with possessing the infinite (or ideal) and the desire for "forbidden" knowledge (total knowledge of the beloved) leads to vampirism. Although the poet describes the loved one as a vampire in these poems, it is she who is objectified ("vamped") by his image of her.

The Lesbian

Another female "monster" which Baudelaire uses thematically is the lesbian. His characterization of the lesbian became one of his strongest influences on the Decadent period. As Walter Benjamin has observed:

> The nineteenth century began to use women without reservation in the production process outside the home. It did so primarily in a primitive fashion by putting them into factories. Consequently, in the course of time masculine traits were bound to manifest themselves in these women.[36]

Speaking of a feminist movement in factories that supplied the February Revolution with a corps of women ("Les Vésuviennes"), Benjamin continued: "Such a change of the feminine habitus [sic] brought out tendencies which were capable of engaging Baudelaire's imagination . . . . The masculinization of women was in keeping with it, so Baudelaire approved of the process."[37]

The lesbian vogue which prevailed from the second third of the nineteenth century to the turn of the century and which was so much a characteristic of the Decadent period in France, came into being with Gautier's *Maupin* (however, Maupin herself is an idealistic, heterosexual and purely feminist Romantic heroine who wears "drag" in order to escape and transcend sexual oppression in her search for personal liberation and the ideal man). Yet as late as 1857, Baudelaire was prosecuted and forced to suppress six of his poems dealing with this forbidden subject; for lesbian love as celebrated by Baudelaire transformed the femme fatale of Romanticism into a monstrous creature—the irredeemable Lesbian—from whom man is forever separated. The poet cursed these monsters of his own creation:

> O demons, monsters, virgins, martyrs, you
> Who trample base reality in scorn,
> Whether as nuns or satyrs you pursue
> The infinite, with cries or tears forlorn.[38]

The Androgyne

In French literature, the ideal of the masculinized woman developed from *Maupin* through Baudelaire, and by the turn of the century it had been refined into the form of the androgyne. Mario Praz said of the novels of Joseph Péladan (1859–1918): "Péladan's work is a veritable encyclopedia of the taste of the Decadents . . . permeated by his . . . sexual obsession, by his Hymn to the Androgyne."[39] This androgynous ideal was the obsession not only of Péladan but the whole Decadent movement. Androgyny was a preoccupation of Baudelaire as well:

> With the hips of Antiope, the torso of a boy,
> So deeply was the one form sprung into the other
> It seemed as if desire had fashioned a new toy.
> Her farded, fawn-brown skin was perfection to either![40]

The ideal of the androgyne (vs. the lesbian monster) was a sexless yet lustful characterization. It is predominant in the paintings of Gustave Moreau and in the novels of Péladan, but it is visible everywhere by the turn of the century; the pale androgyne of Decadence was a refreshing ideal (temptation) after Baudelaire's Amazonian lesbians. Later in this chapter we shall examine the ways in which androgyne, the third sex, emerged from other sexual "monsters" as a symbol of sterility.

Time, Space, Darkness and Light

Our assessment of motifs in Baudelaire would not be complete without considering his interpretations and expression of time, space, darkness and light. A consideration of these phenomena is especially important to a study involved with cinema. As later demonstrated in this chapter, it is within these primary, essential components of poetry that we discover the poet's strongest contribution to the Decadent world view.

Georges Poulet has observed that Baudelaire "painted" his poetic images with "light that is fundamentally dark,"[41] and that Baudelaire's imagery was usually illuminated by artificial light against a "nocturnal background".[42] He explains that "any light that does not emanate directly from the sun seems more beautiful"[43] because "Baudelaire's world is a world of lamps, of chandeliers, of lanterns, of lighting fixtures of all sorts, whose task is to intercept, modify and retransmit light."[44] Baudelaire's light becomes independent of its source; flesh and jewelry seem capable of emanating luminous power: "The moon, a lamp, the hearth, a woman's flesh, are stars whose ever briefer rays usurp the function of the sun."[45]

The images shimmer like nightmares projected on a screen of dark space; this space is the absence of both movement and light: " . . . the motionless background against which the mobile object stands out is nearly always represented in the shape of a dark expanse."[46] The poet complains that:

> I am like a painter whom a mocking God
> Condemns to paint, alas! on darkness.[47]

Two correlatives for light are movement and memory. Often motion is described as "movement of a mobile object that travels in front of a stationary background . . . . Thus psychedelic visions spread their colors, their thrills, their lights on life, whose depths they reveal."[48] Memory, creator of images of the past, is always veiled by the "tears of nostalgia,"[49] and the poet is forever casting backward glances, longing for the ideal past which remains Romantically inaccessible. The nostalgic attitude is distinctly Baudelairean as well as Romantic; but it is the concept of sterility in time and space which places Baudelaire in the Decadent realm of the Romantic movement. As Poulet stated, this negation of time is always expressed as "'everlasting situations'. . . in which future and present are indistinguishable from the past that shapes them."[50] For Baudelaire, time carries a destructive permanence, the invariability of "everlasting situations"; time as a state which persists, coupled with the irrevocable character of fate, results in ennui, impotence, and sterility.

In Baudelaire's vision the suspension of time in a spatial stasis inevitably produces deadly ennui. The will is paralyzed by stagnation. Fate, like the past, eats away at life, producing both impotence and the desire to escape. "As Jean-Paul Sartre has aptly pointed out, Baudelaire was perpetually goaded by a desire to be somewhere else, away from his inertia . . . . "[51] In this flight from himself, the poet tries to see objects exotically, that is to say, as "foreign" objects seen remotely, from the greatest possible distance. He strives to evoke Paradise in his descriptions of space, horizons, and sunsets, longing to recapture past memories and to bask in the rays of their fading glory. His poem "Recueillement" ("Meditation") (1861) describes a sunset;

> . . . Look, the dead years dressed
> in old clothes crowd the balconies of the sky.
> Regret emerges smiling from the sea . . . [52]

In conclusion, let us review the major themes in Baudelaire's work: the crowd motif, representing the importance of the urban stimulus; the theory of *l'art pour l'art* and its espousal of artificiality and objectification; the preoccupation with death and Satanism, and the use of the characters of the dandy, the vampire, the lesbian and the androgyne. In Baudelaire's poetry, the concept of fixed time and space gives rise to nostalgia, obsession, paralysis of the will and ennui. We have also mentioned certain aspects of his technique, "the poetry of shock," and the manner in which he describes luminous images which move against nocturnal space. But before discussing that technique which is often considered to be his most valuable contribution to French poetry—Symbolism—this essay will examine the influences on Baudelaire's thematic content and the development of his themes throughout the literature of the last half of the nineteenth century in France.

The Decadent/Symbolist Aesthetic

Decadence

This section examines Decadent themes in literature and painting. Each of these themes is shown to be, to some extent, Baudelairean. During the last half of the nineteenth century they became refined and united into a pessimistic world view which reflected the national climate. The decadence in society was apparent in France. Social deterioration had set in. George Ross Ridge wrote:

> The Revolutionary and Napoleonic Wars had exhausted the nation with bankruptcy, bloodletting, spleen, despondency. Kantism and positivism crushed Romantic naïveté, and with it much of France's idealism. Science and psychology developed along utilitarian lines and the monied bourgeois has no sympathy for its artists and philosophers.[53]

From the literature of Baudelaire on, the temptations of Paris became an omnipresent theme. George Ross Ridge's exhaustive study, *The Hero in French Decadent Literature*, posed the city of Paris as the major symbol of Decadence:

> It is evil because it divorces men from nature and conditions them to the artificial stimuli of city-living . . . . throughout decadent literature, the protagonist hates his city as he hates his civilization, for all its vices and impurities. . . . in the decadence proper the megalopolis is the modern Babylon—an object of profound and abiding distrust and hatred.[54]

Ridge pointed out a consecutive succession of attitudes and events which can be said to summarize the developments of the Decadent world view:

> The events that produce this world view are linked together in the following way: the megalopolis destroys man's soul, i.e., his *élan vital*, by alienating him from nature. Then modern man becomes weak and effeminate, a cerebral decadent, an impractical aesthete, while the masculinized modern woman usurps his place. Finally, the androgyne emerges as nature's rebellion against the artificialities of Babylon. Nature herself causes this reversal of the sexes in order to impose sterility upon the decadent civilization. Weak and unable to reproduce itself, the world comes to a cataclysmic end. The barbarians, men of nature, will come as the springtime of a new age in a spirit of rejuvenation.[55]

He concluded that urbanization and its overstimulation, artificiality, dandyism, vampirism, lesbianism, androgyny, impotence, and sterility were all aspects that were inseparable from the Decadent aesthetic.

Artificiality. Before we apply Ridge's summary of the Decadent world view to specific works of art or literature, let us consider its various aspects. First, there is the question of "artificiality." One of the distinguishing aspects of Decadence was its emphasis on the perverse and artificial: nature was seen to be inferior to artifice. The cult of artificiality is what separates Decadence from the Romanticism of Jean-Jacques Rousseau's nature cult.

Rousseau and his many followers believed in a strict adherence to nature; but the development of science and industry and the concentration of man in cities had totally cut man off from his traditional ties to nature. The Romantics believed this to be profoundly perverse, a massive contradiction of natural law. This, of course, the Decadents did not refute. It was Rousseau's adherence to the aesthetic doctrine of naturalism which separated them. Baudelaire refuted this doctrine in his *Salon of 1859* in a piece called "The Governance of the Imagination":

> "Nature is but a dictionary", he [Eugène Delacroix] was fond of saying. To understand clearly the meaning implied in this remark, we must bear in mind the numerous and ordinary uses a dictionary is put to. We look up the meaning of words, the derivation of words, the etymology of words; and, finally, we get from a dictionary all the component parts of sentences and ordered narrative. But no one has ever thought of a dictionary as a composition in the poetic sense of the word . . . . Those who have no imagination copy the dictionary, from which arises a very great vice, the vice of banality, to which are particularly exposed those . . . whose specialty lies nearest to external nature . . . . [56]

This cult of naturalism had been attacked many times before in the novels of de Sade. These attacks showed how nature had become so identified with what was normal and virtuous, that a renunciation of nature (as the naturalists saw it) was necessarily an indication of the abnormal and perverse. Mario Praz, in his survey of Romantic literature, traced the prevalence of sensuality and perversity throughout Romanticism. He stated:

> The Marquis de Sade . . . reversed the . . . ethical theory [of] Jean-Jacques [Rousseau]. "Everything is good, everything is the work of God" become in him "Everything is evil, everything is the work of Satan". It is therefore necessary to practice vice because it conforms to the laws of nature . . . . Evil is the axis of the universe. [57]

As A.E. Carter has stated:

> . . . the abnormal becomes a proof of man's superiority to natural law, a demonstration of free will, an "artificiality" which, although more lurid than face-paint or dyed hair, is of the same order. [58]

> This is the main idea behind the cult of artificiality.

The novelist Joris-Karl Huysmans is an exemplar of the hatred for nineteenth-century civilization, that civilization which flourished with such a "perverse" vitality. In *A rebours* (1884), the seminal novel of Decadence, the hero, Duc Jean Floressas des Esseintes (an exhausted survivor of the French aristocracy) is driven by his desire to escape from the squalor and banality of the contemporary materialist world. Duc des Esseintes travels in imagined time and space through the exquisite orchestration of his senses. His desire to transcend contemporary civilization drives him into building a cocoon-like hermitage (riddled with sumptuous little environments), in which his sole preoccupation is to indulge and stimulate his senses. In order to achieve this, he relies more and more heavily on distorting nature; he encrusts the shell of a giant tortoise with inlaid gems; slowly this "crawling footstool" dies from the experiment. He plans an elaborate trip to London, but by now, however, he is overwhelmed by his own imagination. He no longer has the strength to make the journey, for he has used up his energy in imagining it. Reverie (ideality), he knows, is infinitely more satisfying than action (reality). This incident exemplifies the similar polarity of the Decadent and Romantic world views: the imagination is more perfect than the material world. Des Esseintes's desire to replace actuality with an imagined ideal (by traveling through his senses, his imagination) is a direct manifestation of his love for the artificial, and basic to the Decadent stance. A paralysis of the will is the price des Esseintes pays for going "against the grain" and tampering with nature. The novel ends with a penitent des Esseintes gloomily embracing Catholicism.

Another novel of Decadent literature, one which illustrates the most elaborate use of time and space "exoticism" (displacement or transposition) is Octave Mirbeau's *Le Jardin des supplices* (*The Torture Garden*) (1899). Here the unnamed hero and the heroine Clara seek relief from the ennui and corruption of European civilization. As Clara explains to the hero:

> In China life is free, joyous, complete, unconventional, unprejudiced, lawless . . . at least for us. No other limits to liberty than yourself . . . or to love, than the triumphant variety of your desire. Europe and its hypocritical civilization is a lie . . . . You live attached in a cowardly fashion to moral and social conventions you despise, condemn, and know lack all foundation. It is the permanent contradiction between your ideas and desires and all the dead formalities and vain pretenses of your civilization which makes you lose . . . all joy of life and all feeling of personality, because at every moment they suppress and restrain and check the free play of your powers. That's the poisoned and mortal wound of the civilized world.[59]

Mirbeau did not deny the existence of love, but it had now been transformed from ideal Romantic love to a form whose expression was now firmly rooted in the flesh. We can see the powerful influence of de Sade when Mirbeau states, "Murder is born of love, and love attains its greatest intensity in murder."[60] The hero and Clara go to the heroine's home in the inland city of Canton in China. Their ceaseless quest to extend the limits of experience and fulfill what they believe are their natural desires leads to obsessive cruelty; they frequently visit the public execution and torture grounds, "The Garden of Punishments." The scenes describing their visits to this exotic but revolting spot reveal a penultimate refinement of sadism in Mirbeau's China; for all its exotic allure, China had developed a culture replete in monstrous perversities: " . . . the dead enriched it by their slow decomposition, and besides, in no other place . . . could a land richer in natural mould be found."[61] There is a tropical mingling of torture and horticulture, blood with flowers. The poisonous aspects of the European world were no less fatal than the exotic traditions of torture and love in China where "Art . . . consists in knowing how to kill, according to the rites of beauty . . . . "[62]

The Decadent characteristics of dandyism, narcissism, sterility, algolagnia, and time/space exoticism all may be considered distortions of "natural" laws and, as such, perverse extensions of the cult of artificiality. Throughout Decadent literature, modern man—the Decadent hero—proclaims his preference for artifice over nature. In his *Les Paradis artificiels* (*The Artificial Paradises*) (1860), Baudelaire began with an essay on "Le goût de l'infini." It is this "taste for infinity," according to Baudelaire, which leads man to seek artificial means of obtaining the "mysterious effects and morbid pleasures" of what he calls the *"artificial Ideal."*[63] But Baudelaire went on to write of "the punishments that inevitably result from their [excitants] prolonged use; and finally, of the very immorality involved in such a pursuit of an artificial ideal."[64] *Paradis artificiels* proclaims a pessimistic faith based on redemption through sin, for, as Edouard Rodite pointed out in his foreword to *Paradis*:

> . . . the individual cannot achieve his own salvation through mere innocence and ignorance or inexperience of sin, but requires an experience of evil and redemption from it through contrition, remorse, and the will to save himself from his own past errors and aberrations.[65]

The hero of Decadent literature seeks to be overpowered, conquered by his senses. The cult of artificiality was now self-consciously perverse, and here again, it was sharply distinguished from Romanticism.

The Decadent dandy. The hero of the Decadent world created a role for himself which perfectly suited a contempt for his civilization and the demands of artificiality; he patterned himself on a variation of Baudelaire's dandy. Baudelaire first wrote of Dandyism in the 1850s, and by the 1860s his concepts had been incorporated into the Decadent stance (remaining influential through the 1890s); Dandyism became an expression of disdain for one's own time.

In contrast to the heroes of Huysmans and Mirbeau, Baudelaire's dandy, however frustrated by the situations imposed upon him by modern life, remains in command both of himself and his environment. We can pinpoint the major difference between the Decadent dandy (whom we shall see to be a victim of his own era) and Baudelaire's dandy by analyzing two statements from Baudelaire's *Journaux intimes*:

> We are weighed down every moment by the conception and the sensation of Time. And there are but two means of escaping and forgetting this nightmare: Pleasure and Work. Pleasure consumes us. Work strengthens us. . . . [66]
>
> . . . .
>
> Desire for Pleasure attaches us to the Present. Care for our safety makes us dependent upon the Future.
>
> He who clings to Pleasure, that is, to the Present, makes me think of a man rolling down a slope who, in trying to grasp hold of some bushes, tears them up and carries them with him in his fall. [67]

In an attempt to escape the pressures of the age, the modern Decadent dandy, who, by definition, had to be a "man of leisure" and "love work,"[68] now became a creature wholly indifferent to intellectual interests; his sole preoccupation was now the vicious indulgence of his animal passions (des Esseintes is the perfect example). In Baudelaire's above enumeration of the possible means of escape, he later stated, "The more we employ one of these means, the more the other will inspire us with repugnance."[69] The modern dandies were now creatures of the senses, wholly engaged in pursuit of more and more extreme sensory indulgences; and, as Baudelaire predicted, work grew to be a more and more repulsive prospect for them.

The concept of Decadent Dandyism now lay between artificiality and pure sensuality. The dandy, a product of the megalopolis, found himself incapable of functioning in this new world. He had totally absented himself from it; yet, by losing control of himself and his environment, he grew more passive and finally became but another victim of the Decadent era. Baudelaire's dandy was supremely suited for the conditions of the life he had to endure; he remained untouched by its corruption, still able to take advantage of his situation.

We can see a condemnation of the Decadent dandy in a passage from Baudelaire's *Paradis*:

> In effect, every man who does not accept the conditions of life, sells his soul. It is sinister to seize the situation—the sinister relation—which exists between the Satanical Creations of the Poets and the living creatures who devote themselves to Excitants. Man has desired to become God, and now he has found that he has, in virtue of an uncontrollable moral law, fallen lower than his real nature.[70]

When one remembers that Baudelaire believed, "To be a great man and a

saint *by one's own standards*, that is all that matters,"[71] and that "Evil is done without effort, *naturally*, it is the working of fate; good is always the product of an art,"[72] one can observe that the only similarity between Baudelaire's dandy and the Decadent hero is simply one of their elegant outward appearance. It is plain to see the former as hero and the latter as helpless victim of human nature.

The basic themes discussed thus far—pessimism, artificiality, Dandyism—combined into an attitude toward woman which was the logical antithesis of Romantic love. The Decadent artist scorned nature and "natural" functions; he held vitality in contempt. He therefore reversed the vital role of the Romantic hero into the passive dandy and cast woman into a new part: the femme fatale. Decadent heroines became "unnaturally" aggressive and masculinized even as the Decadent hero grew more and more passive. No longer the Fatal Man of the Romantics, he had given way to the Fatal Woman.

The femme fatale: the vamp, the "creature," and Salomé. In "Les Métamorphosis du vampire" ("Metamorphosis of the Vampire") from *Fleurs*, Baudelaire portrayed modern man and woman in a manner that obsessed writers of the French Decadence. Modern man was shown as weak and effeminate, consumed by modern woman who is a vampire or femme fatale. "Their love is a passionate death-struggle in which the active female, like a spider, destroys the passive male."[73]

For the heroine Clara, of *Le Jardin des supplices*, "Love and death are the same thing!"[74] Her adventures as a sado-masochistic nymphomaniac defy description. Like the Chinese torture gardens, she thrives on incredible displays of violence, pain, and death. This principle of demonic energy that drives the heroine is the essential characteristic in the portrait of woman in Decadent literature. The women described by Baudelaire and Paul Verlaine are satanic vampires who have usurped man's historic role and broken the natural bonds of Romantic love.

Praz traces the literary lineage of the femme fatale back through the Romantics to Matthew Gregory Lewis's *The Monk* (1796).[75] The primitive literary origins of the femme fatale were in the gypsy girls and witches of ancient folk tales and myths; but she makes her grand entrance in Prosper Mérimée's satire *Une Femme est un diable* (1825). (Mérimée's *Notre-Dame de Paris* [1831] set the fatal *allumeuse* Carmen against the landscape of Spain, combining the exotic and erotic in character and place in much the same way as did Gustave Flaubert's *Salammbô* [1862]). She was, from then onward, quite often of Spanish and Creole origins, as was Baudelaire's mistress Jeanne Duval. The femme fatale was passionate, socially dangerous and self-destructive. Her conquest of the hero usually involved suicidal and murderous tactics.

The mythical origins of the fatal woman hark back to the Medusa and the Sphinx. More mythical beasts than goddesses, they symbolize the ancient "fatal" aspects of the woman as animal (e.g., the Harpies or the Gorgons). Philippe Jullian stated:

> The Sphinx is even more awe-inspiring than the Medusa, for she possesses the faculty of thought.
>
> She is a promise of the Ideal, with the body of a carnivorous beast.[76]

Gustave Moreau, the Symbolist painter, obtained notable success in the 1864 Salon Exhibit in Paris with a painting of *Oedipe et le Sphinx*. The hero Oedipus and the monster-heroine exchange gazes; she is perched on his chest, her rear paws dug in dangerously close to his groin. Rather than representing conflict between good and evil, the two appear as though they are locked in a battle of the sexes.

Salomé is usually considered to be the ultimate Decadent/Symbolist heroine. She embodied the dual aspects of sublime Beauty and supreme Evil, and, as such, became a favorite subject in the painting and literature of the epoch. In these portrayals of her, we encounter the themes of narcissism and inertia which were so strongly set forth in the second (or "death") edition of *Fleurs*. Though immortalized by Flaubert in *Salammbô*, she was established as the Decadent Muse by Huysmans. Her combination of desire and death suited his morbid imagination; he seized upon Salomé as an embodiment of the lust and evil incarnate in woman. Moreau's paintings of Salomé, as she danced before King Herod or stood transfixed before the head of John the Baptist, became a fixed apparition of the femme fatale, the "unnatural" woman who was such a characteristic of the fin de siècle.

Huysmans, through the character of des Esseintes, describes her in Moreau's painting *Salomé Dancing Before Herod* (1876):

> . . . the symbolic incarnation of world-old Vice, the goddess of immortal Hysteria, the Curse of Beauty supreme above all other beauties by the cataleptic spasm that stirs her flesh and steels her muscles,—a monstrous beast of the Apocalypse, indifferent, irresponsible, insensible, poisoning . . . .[77]

At a later point in the novel, des Esseintes, having purchased a slim volume of Mallarmé's poetry, recalls once again Moreau's image of Salomé:

> Involuntarily, he lifted his eyes and looked. There gleamed the never-to-be-forgotten outlines of her shape; she lived again, recalling to his lips those weird, sweet words that Mallarmé puts in her mouth:
>
> ". . . O mirror! / chill water-pool frozen by ennui, within thy frame, / how many times,

and for hours long, tortured / by dreams and searching my memories that are / like dead leaves under the glassy surface that covers thy depths profound, / have I seen myself in these like a far-off shadow! / But, horror! Of evenings, in thy cruel fountain, / have I known the bare nudity of my broken vision."[78]

Remaining "fatal" and alluring as ever, she was now revealed, in a sense, as Mallarmé's poem *Hérodiade* (1898) depicted her: the narcissistic virgin, anguished and sterile, trapped alone before her mirror. Hérodiade knew that beauty was death:

> . . . a kiss would kill me
> if beauty were not death . . . [79]

Mallarmé's glacial figure may have been suggested by the sonnet of Baudelaire which ended:

> Her eyes are carved of minerals pure and cold,
> And in her strange symbolic nature where
> An angel mingles with the sphinx of old,
>
> Where all is gold and steel and light and air,
> For ever, like a vain star, unafraid
> Shines the cold hauteur of the sterile maid.[80]

Sterility: Androgyny. The idea of active inaction was taken much further by Stéphane Mallarmé, whose poetry was obsessed with the themes of impotence and sterility. In his poems the symbols of sterility are everywhere, as Ridge has pointed out: "the frozen lake that has captured the swan, the glittering hoarfrost and the transparent ice, the pale agony and the cold dream."[81] For Mallarmé, the old poetic themes of life and vigor had vanished. Sterility was transformed into the supreme ideal.

His poem *Hérodiade* deals with an extreme form of narcissism; there is little action save the dancer's sterile contemplation of her own beauty. *Hérodiade* reads as though Mallarmé had written it as a variation of Baudelaire's maxim "The Dandy should . . . live and sleep in front of a mirror."[82] Hérodiade, like the dandy, unites narcissism, paralysis, stillness, and sterility. As Ridge has stated:

> As the Romantic hero passes into a new hero-type, one which is best called "decadent," cerebral figures begin to appear with alarming frequency. In Baudelaire's *La Fanfarlo* Samuel Cramer presages the new man as he tries to lash himself into movement every morning. Action, the young dandy says, is scarcely worth the effort.[83]

The hero, his energies sapped by overindulgence, is increasingly trapped in languor and sterility.

A third sex emerges in Decadent literature. It is the androgyne, which may be a man with feminine characteristics or a woman with masculine traits. The androgyne may be a transvestite, a pervert, or asexual, but the sexual identity is unimportant in the Decadent world view; the Decadent writers stressed that the androgyne was biologically sterile. It incarnated what was antinatural in its most obvious form and it was thus a refutation of sex, love, and life. The androgyne signaled the ultimate in sterility, the end of civilization. Homosexuality was a latent theme, but the androgyne was an omnipresent theme throughout the novels of the 1890s. Carter has stated:

> Sexual perversions, in fact, are the chief ingredients in all these works—usually appearing as androgynism and Lesbianism, both described as symptoms of Decadence. By the eighties, Romanticism's *mal du siècle* had become androgynism ... "La Maladie du siècle."[84]

The Decadent hero is a man who, like society, is incurably ill, and, like civilization, is slowly dying. And as Ridge has stated: "Death is his aesthetic solution to the riddle of life: death is ultimately necessary because his life has no further artistic interest. Death is the finis of a work of art."[85]

Symbolism

How did the Decadent artist portray pessimism and sterility? What techniques best expressed narcissism and androgyny? Decadent aesthetics were the aesthetics of Symbolism, and it is, in fact, impossible to separate Symbolist themes and techniques from Decadent themes and techniques. According to Alfred Garwin Engstrom:

> s[ymbolism] differs from historical Fr[ench] romanticism in its greater subtlety and preoccupation with the inner life and in its general avoidance of sentimentality, rhetoric, narration, direct statement, description, public and political themes, and overt didacticism of any kind .... Symbolist poetry is a poetry of indirection, in which objects tend to be suggested rather than named [e.g., Paul Verlaine referring to a cloud, writes, "The black rock"], or to be used primarily for an evocation of mood. Ideas may be important, but are characteristically presented obliquely through a variety of symbols and must be apprehended largely by intuition and feeling. Symbolist poets use words for their magical suggestiveness ... one of their essential aims is to arouse response beyond the level of ordinary consciousness .... For the symbolists the power of the Word goes far beyond ordinary denotative verbal limits through suggestive developments in syntax and interrelated images and through what may be termed the "phonetic s[ymbolism]" of musicality and connotative sound-relationships.[86]

The following represents the operation of this system in poetry:

Symbolist Metaphor: $X = Y = Z$, but only Z is given in the poem itself.

Specific Object	General Essence	Specific Exotic Equivalent
dew	water	globule
rose	flower	orchid

Thus: "dew on a rose" becomes in the poem "the globuled orchid."

The Symbolist movement developed first in the literary arts and only later became evident in painting. For Baudelaire, the exemplar of Symbolist poets, it was imagination that produced order, structure, and significance. It did so by defining various relationships between material and spiritual realities, or intimations of what he termed "l'analogie universelle" ("the universal analogy").[87] Part of Baudelaire's theory of correspondences included the idea that experiences normally associated with one sense might find an echo in a different sense. In the *Salon of 1846*, Baudelaire quoted Ernst Theodor Amadeus Hoffman from the latter's *Kreisleriana*, explaining that he believed it best expressed his own thoughts on the matter:

> Not only in dreams and in the free association of ideas (which phenomenon often comes just before sleep) but also when fully awake, listening to music, I find an analogy and a close union between colours, sounds and scents. I have the impression all these things have been created by one and the same ray of light, and that they are destined to unite in a wonderful concert. The scent of brown and red marigolds especially produces a magical effect on my being. I fall into a profound reverie and then hear as though from afar, the solemn, deep notes of the oboe.[88]

As Engstrom wrote of Baudelaire:

> His sonnet *Correspondances* describes man moving through a "forest of symbols" familiarly related to his existence, and proclaims two kinds of interrelated *correspondences*: (1) those (in the manner of Swedenborg and the great mystics generally since Plato) between material world and spiritual realities, and (2) those between the different sense modalities [*synaesthesia*].[89]

Mallarmé, who admired and was greatly influenced by Baudelaire's work, stressed the importance of not describing directly, and the importance of the sounds of words and their musicality. In 1886, the Greek/ French poet Jean Moréas made clear the aim of his art in the *Manifesto of Symbolism*:

> . . . the idea should not make its appearance deprived of the sumptuous trappings of external analogies, for the essential character of Symbolist art consists of never going straight to the conception of the idea itself.[90]

The Symbolist poets were greatly concerned with the dreams of unreality. They admitted that they were incapable of perceiving or experiencing a static reality and their verse, therefore, was purposefully suggestive. They could only suggest certain attributes of the thing-in-itself, not recreate it. Although they were highly descriptive, reality for the Symbolist poets was frail and indefinite because it was so transmutable. As Ridge believes, the Decadent/Symbolist introspection was not "simply a refusal to communicate with the world, but also a self-preoccupied attempt to create another world through the cult of *sensationalism*."[91]

Like Huysmans's des Esseintes, the Decadent hero was a relativist. He lived in a Symbolist world of sensually perceived phenomena; one of changing forms, not in an immutable universe of eternal forms. A perception of the world as a vision of changing sensual phenomena produced a written style that was full of luxurious sophistication, what A.E. Carter has called the "glamour of syntax." In Bernard Weinberg's words, "the syntax of the sentence [was] . . . distorted and contorted for the purpose of rendering the meaning more subtle and the emphasis more forceful."[92] As the reader's senses had been dulled by continuous excitement, only the strongest stimulations could now affect him.

A Decadent/Symbolist writer could have no explicit vision of a world except as an object of sensation recorded in style. This represented a clear reversal of classical values. Havelock Ellis, in his preface to *A rebours*, elaborates:

> Technically, a decadent style is only such in relation to classic style. It is simply a further development of a classic style, a further specialization . . . .
>
> But the best early statement on the meaning of decadence in style—though doubtless inspired by Baudelaire—was furnished by Gautier in 1868 in the course of the essay on Baudelaire . . . .
>
> "The poet of the 'Fleurs du Mal' loved what is improperly called the style of decadence, and which is nothing else but art arrived at the point of extreme maturity yielded by the slanting suns of aged civilizations: an ingenious complicated style, full of shades and of research, constantly pushing back the boundaries of speech, borrowing from all the technical vocabularies, taking colour from all palettes and notes from all keyboards, struggling to render what is most inexpressible in thought, what is vague and most elusive in the outlines of form, listening to translate the subtle confidence of neurosis, the dying confessions of passion grown depraved, and the strange hallucinations of the obsession that is turning to madness."[93]

Decadent experiments with syntax included the use of sustained metaphors, epithets, and neologisms; all of these can be associated with the cult of artificiality and the deliberate control of the dandy. To let oneself go on the wings of inspiration was too natural, too Romantic; the Decadent/Symbolist style was deliberate and artificial. It expressed an aesthetic which demanded a more complex, more highly colored style to replace the "natural" simplicities and platitudes of the past. It was Huysmans, deliberate and relentless, who carried the theory and practice of Decadent style to the farthest point, through an intentional distortion of syntax:

> Huysmans' vocabulary is vast, his images, whether remote or familiar, always daring— "dragged," in the words of one critic, "by the hair or feet, down the worm-eaten staircase of terrified Syntax . . . ."[94]

Although Symbolist techniques first appeared in poetry, Symbolist painters eventually exerted a major influence on the Decadent writers of the 1880s and 1890s. We have seen, for example, that Huysmans's hero des Esseintes, was greatly excited by the work of Gustave Moreau. John Milner has noted that:

> In Gustave Moreau's art, Huysmans was seeking a modern pictorial form appropriate to the perverse tastes of Des Esseintes. This is an important example of the search by literary intellectuals for a pictorial art form to correspond to literary Decadence.[95]

Moreau's Symbolist paintings will be used in this survey to point up analogous themes and styles in Baudelairean Cinema. It would seem useful, therefore, to review some terminology of the movement, as traced by Philippe Jullian, in his article, "Dreams of Decadence.":

> In the early days of the movement these painters like to call themselves "idealists" or "painters of the soul," rather than Symbolists; nevertheless, the term Symbolist survived since their art is virtually inseparable from the works of the Symbolist writers . . . . Symbolism is rather a style, a certain preciousness, a particular view of the world, even an ethic. The nearest comparable phenomenon is Mannerism, with its oddities and rejection of nature . . . .[96]

Among the Symbolist painters, Moreau's work is thought to be most representative of Decadent sensibilities; "Moreau's vision of Byzantium and the protagonists of ancient myth is pervaded by pessimism, languor, and the cult of death and melancholy recognized in his work by the literary decadents."[97]

The nineteenth-century Symbolist writers and painters elevated technique into something more than aesthetic perception. The technique itself became an ethic which was inseparable from the Decadent world view with its pessimism, languor, and its melancholy.

The following chapter demonstrates how nineteenth-century French Decadence and the Symbolist aesthetic reappeared during the 1960s in the Baudelairean Cinema.

Analogies between Decadence/Symbolism and the Baudelairean Cinema

Warhol and Pop Art

Decadence—as it existed in nineteenth-century France—includes six major characteristics: dissatisfaction with civilization, pessimism, dandyism, sterility, a view of women as the destructive femme fatale, and androgyny. How does the Baudelairean Cinema reflect these characteristics? Where do we find twentieth-century attitudes and techniques analogous to the original Baudelairean era? The Baudelairean filmmakers were, first of all, associated to one degree or another with a major artistic movement of the American 1960s—Pop Art—and it is the Pop Art movement which offers the first and most obvious analogies to the earlier Decadence.

The dissatisfaction with civilization which preoccupied so many writers of the French Decadent era (Mirbeau, Huysmans, Lautréamont) resurfaced as an expression of urban and industrial malaise and was developed to the highest degree seventy years later in the Pop Art movement. The Pop Art movement was primarily graphic and its subject matter usually included images of mass-produced, consumer goods. The movement reflected and criticized the American economy by reproducing images of mass-produced objects and images used in advertising. The Pop artist believed his subjects to be statements in themselves, ready-made symbols of our culture; the artist merely isolated the subjects from their surroundings so that they caught our attention in a new context.

"Consumerism" in a capitalist society is perhaps most clearly articulated in Andy Warhol's silkscreen series of dollar bills (1962). In this "portrait" of money, the bills are simply arranged side-by-side. Through repetition, the subject matter gains no additional value to the spectator beyond its value as a symbol. As a symbol, the dollar bill is, of course, available to millions of Americans, and this common visual availability is reemphasized when it is repeated and framed because the object (dollars) becomes the subject of "art" (*framed*, arranged, dollars). The repetition, framing, and exhibiting of

American dollar bills renders the symbolic significance of money impotent. Norman Mailer has written that "Money is authority stamped on emptiness."[1] Warhol's dollar bill silkscreen illustrates the truth of Mailer's statement. The "subjectified" money or the art work goes through a reobjectification when we examine it as a piece of art which has greater economic value than the amount actually shown in the silkscreen. The dollar is robbed of its uniqueness, as well as its economic significance. The dollar, as a symbol of money and power, repeated, framed, and displayed becomes one of civilization's static artifacts; as art, its uselessness is emphasized, it becomes an insignificant, banal, and repulsive object. The dollar, as empty artifact, reflects the banality of the society which produced it. It is the *image* of the dollar, not the economic resonances of the dollar, which is emphasized in Warhol's silkscreen.

Finally, the symbol of money is drained of all past significance of money-as-economic power because of the overt ambiguity of the visual codes or messages operating at once within the same concept. These would include three basic messages: (1) money-as-money, (2) money-as-art, (3) art-as-money.

True to Decadent form, Warhol sapped the economic energy from one of civilization's artifacts, the dollar bill. He had other methods for demythologizing other "heavily charged" and highly significant symbols of American culture: for Warhol, painting is "the reproduction of an art work which has been *designed to be reproduced*."[2] Even a partial list of Warhol's works between 1960 and 1962 is enough to illustrate his preoccupation with mass-produced objects: 1960, comic-strip paintings; 1961, early fruit tins, Coca-Cola labels, bottles, newspaper front pages, dancestep diagrams, soup cans; 1962, multiple-image Cokes, stamps, do-it-yourself paintings, painted soup cans, and pencil drawings of soup cans, crushed, stacked, full and empty, with dollar bills flowing from the top, etc.

Warhol presents a commercialized view of America. He began with commercial objects such as postage stamps, Coke bottles, Campbell's soup cans, S and H green stamps, and money. When put in an artistic context, these objects of our daily life become symbols of our existence. As such, the repetition of the soup cans, or Coke bottles in Warhol's work give a feeling of the redundancy and shallowness of life in America. It is laughably pathetic that these objects are indeed very real symbols of our culture. These are the profits, the spoils of a good life. They are seductive, as is the material well-being of America; one can't help but read the labels and look for a difference, but it doesn't matter if it is black bean or chicken gumbo, it is all the same.

Warhol took this concept further when he applied it to human tragedy. His silkscreens of the *Death and Disaster Series* (1963–1964) appear to have come from the newspapers. The tragedy is commercial. Warhol spreads it, multiplied on the canvas so that one can view it coldly, objectively, passively. One scans the repetition of the images of disaster looking for a clearer picture of the maimed dead bodies of the car crash. It is paralyzed hysteria, safe and controlled. Control and paralysis epitomize Warhol's dandyism. In each disaster he can scrutinize intense human experience and remain detached, cool, and objective. Warhol is obsessed with intensity in human experience, yet he must always control it, keep it at a safe distance. He wants to experience through other people, so that he runs no risks. Then he breaks down that experience into his terms, so that he can deal with it. The repetition in the *Disaster Series* is the same as the repetition of Coke bottles—a manifestation of American life and Americans. Warhol's is a vision of people as objects, human tragedy as an object in American culture.

Warhol's obsession with uniquely twentieth-century imagery (car crashes, Coke bottles), uniquely twentieth-century sex symbols (Marilyn Monroe, Elizabeth Taylor), and with death (the Electric Chair silkscreens, the Condemned Man silkscreens) reflects his condemnation of society. These works are just as strong an expression of pessimistic dissatisfaction with civilization as Huysmans's *A rebours*.

In making a general comparison between the pessimism in Pop Art and the pessimism of the nineteenth-century Decadent artists, there are notable differences. The French Decadents thought of the world as being overtaken by artificiality and moving toward ruin. There is a sense of dissipation and sensual indulgence as civilization approaches the Apocalypse. Several Pop artists (Claes Oldenburg, Wayne Thiebaud, James Rosenquist), however, tend to take a more exuberant and humorous view of life. This is, of course, a generalization, because not all Pop artists' works are in complete agreement. But, taken as a whole, irony, often tempered by humor, seems to override any feelings of impending doom. Of all Pop works, Warhol's *Disaster Series* comes closest to the depiction of a civilization destroying itself.

In addition to their dissatisfaction with civilization, Pop artists also shared the nineteenth-century Decadent artists' passion for artificiality. The very subject matter of Pop Art is manufactured by machines, and Pop Art often has the look of being "untouched by human hands," a look provoked by the assembly line process of American industry. Pop Art borrowed Big Business advertising techniques in which the image designed for the container is more important than the product contained. The pictorial language of Pop Art is the stereotyped, cliché image borrowed from advertising, and the consumer-item objects depicted in Pop Art are the very objects which prevent modern man from making contact with nature.[3] They are Pop Art's glorified artifacts, objects which have been "aestheticized" into subjects: commercial objects transformed into objets d'art.

The general themes common to Pop Art and the French Decadent movement appear with specific force in the Baudelairean Cinema. Perhaps the most obvious heir to the Decadent tradition among Baudelairean film-makers is Warhol—the most notorious artist of the entire Pop Art era:

> Warhol is the greatest living inheritor of that creature of style Baudelaire so flawlessly described [the dandy] . . . . Baudelaire describes a man who lives only through an image of himself. The dandy is an *envisioned* man . . . . So it is with Warhol.[4]

The sense one gets of Warhol is of a shy self-contained voyeur who must deal with over-stimulation in modern life. His method of dealing with it is to keep things at a distance by artistically invalidating them. We have seen how he even invalidates art (at least within the context of his work). He "creates" nothing. He uses "found" objects (reproduceables) from our culture as subject matter, and his process is silkscreening which he doesn't even necessarily do himself. Warhol's genius lay in his sense of the 1960s, his timing. He was "on top" of the New York scene; he was a catalyst for what was happening then in painting, theatre, and film. As he moved into film, he became responsible for a merger between the art world and the underground street life of New York. He ruled that world as ruthlessly as a fascist dictator, or a Hollywood movie czar. Some people became stars, some died. Warhol was always at a safe distance.

> Warhol's own solution to the narcissistic dilemma is so simple that it is positively breathtaking. It has been to absent himself as conspicuously as possible. He has joined the dandy's strategy with that of the voyeur, and elevated the conjunction to a principle of being. Predictably enough, as the ultimate voyeur, Warhol has surrounded himself with exhibitionists.[5]

His early films offer a different approach to the problem of dealing with over-stimulation in modern life. He opted to keep his distance from his subjects; he chose subjects that were intrinsically boring; and he chose to show them "frozen"; that is, his camera was static. Rather than finding essence through repetition of one moment in time, Warhol's early camera stared unaltered, unmoved at an object fixed in space for a long period of time. This technique lays activities bare. One follows the subject through banal action, the action is always banal; one senses time passing, so heavily one feels each minute.

In the early films Warhol exhaustively examined some relatively simple, or common subjects: *Sleep, Kiss, Haircut, Eat, Blow Job,* and *Empire.* The films are notorious; they were made to be talked about, but few people actually saw them. It is probably not necessary to see them. They are concept films, and, as concepts, they are valuable. Warhol challenges the very notion of art and its subject matter in these films by taking a commonplace event (of the sort to which we would not give a second thought) and elongating its duration, thus making us painfully aware of every aspect of it. His method makes us aware that we expect something to happen; we want plots, conclusions. Warhol gives us a passage of time or a banal activity and he presents it as art. Our boredom is turned into a comment on our cultural pre-conditioning: our expectation of cinematic stimulation.

"Moldy" Art

Warhol's contemporaries—Ken Jacobs and Jack Smith—turned fear of overstimulation into a full-time preoccupation. They were disgusted with civilization in general and urban American man in particular. Ken Jacobs said:

> We were obsessed by the quality of failure. My film, *Star Spangled to Death*, is a testament to failure. Jack and I had a horror of life, a deep disgust with existence. Jack indulged in it spitefully, he would plunge himself into the garbage of life. He had a hilarious and horrifying willingness to "revel in the dumps," to create some sort of "garbage culture."
>
> Pop Art was a thing we hated. In 1958 Allan Kaprow exhibited the first "Happenings." We said, "Hey, this guy's doing our stuff," but doing it badly. Kaprow's interpretation of our "Human Wreckage" aesthetic seemed too decorative, meaningless and cute. It lacked terror. I remember Jack's place on Sixth Street, like a horrid nineteen-thirties von Sternbergian set, cluttered up with signs of poverty. We shared a terrific hunger for movies because at this time there was not much to see. We lusted after nineteen-forties films by Universal—especially the ones with Dan Duryea; these had atmosphere, a *mise-en-scène* about them and a nostalgic fantasy atmosphere. We both loved the Andrews Sisters, for instance; I lived in the thirties, Jack in the forties. We suffered from nostalgia already, saw Hollywood as a seedy garbage heap. We saw the waste of some low-budget personalities . . . . For *Star Spangled to Death* I built a set and Jack and Jerry Simms were given chaotic patterns of destruction to enact. I would build into the set "created situations" they would then break up . . . . Like the end of *Zabriskie Point* with the exploding garbage, we had that same sort of interest in breaking things; revelations would come from breaking things open. All life was garbage, hopelessness; we were disgusted by the price of existence, in a puke from suffering. Our joy was dependent on the suffering and sorrows of the world.[6]

In his article "Jack Smith, or the End of Civilization," Jonas Mekas described one of Smith's "Destruction of Atlantis" happenings at Smith's New York loft:

> . . . only here, in this downtown loft, somewhere at the very end of all the empty and dead and gray downtown streets, was this huge junk set and these end-of-civilization activities, these happenings, this theatre. I began getting a feeling, it resembled more and more the final burial ceremonies, the final burial rites of the capitalist civilization, competitive

civilization, these were the magic burial grounds and the burial rites of all the corruption, comfort and money and good living and free gifts of the world that was now asleep, at 2 A.M., only Jack Smith was still alive, a madman, the high priest of the ironical burial grounds, administering last services here alone and by himself . . . .

. . . at the moment it all became part of the huge sadness of the burial grounds, the end of civilization sadness, part of the plan, part of the human wreckage, all prearranged by Jack, the Madman of Grand Street . . . . whatever anybody does to destroy his art falls into his art, becomes part of the huge collage, no matter what they do. He prearranged the music and the whole set so that it absorbs everything—exactly like the end of the civilization itself which it seemed to portray—yes, this set became like this culture that seems to absorb everything and everybody—a huge dumping grounds, and open mouth of graveyards—[7]

Jack Smith's films, slide-shows and happenings are all expressions of civilized man's exhaustion from the ceaseless flow of urban stimuli. As in the Decadent era in France, this kind of exhaustion is the result of habitual overstimulation. One of the working titles of one of Jack Smith's latest films is, in fact, *Overstimulated*. Mekas singles out Smith as a "madman" dancing on the ruins of urban civilization, but apocalyptic visions are also strongly evident in Baudelairean films made by Kenneth Anger and Andy Warhol. Although Anger and Warhol express their visions in quite different styles from Jack Smith or Ron Rice, they also use apocalyptic images, and their themes concern the quest for energy through stimulation.

Kenneth Anger's thematic quest for energy appears throughout *Inauguration of the Pleasure Dome* (1954–1966) in which Shiva repeatedly invokes personal power. Beyond magic and visions, Anger, in his quest, was also preoccupied with "the thing that goes"—the machine. His films *Kustom Kar Kommandos* (1965–1966) and *Scorpio Rising* (1966) present idealized images of machines, transformed by montage and photography into totems. Andy Warhol has also repeatedly stressed his admiration for machines and their superiority over human beings: "I'd like to be a machine, wouldn't you?"[8]

The aesthetic of artificiality which was so much a part of the art for art's sake cult of the nineteenth century resurfaces in Jack Smith's "high" exoticism, a term we use here to mean a *less* serious attitude, a more frivolous or indulgent attitude. But in its own way, the Decadent aesthetic of Jack Smith's "moldy glamour" or "pasty art" is a terrifying damnation of urban civilization in the twentieth century:

Moldy is something that is very lush and gaudy and colorful and primitive and a bit old, but it could also be very new and have all those qualities or essences, like fans or feathers or costumes or even make-up on people . . . to create a sort of moldy effect like orange and pink . . . . [moldy things] are imperfect and ugly and this is very rich material to work with, especially the artifacts of the recent past.[9]

This recalls Baudelaire's phrase "la phosphorescence de la pourriture" ("the phosphorescence of decay").[10] In discussing Smith's *Normal Love*, playwright Ronald Tavel explains the work's relationship to Smith's concept of "pasty art":

> Since *Creatures*, Smith has been engaged in the masterful editing of *Normal Love* and attempting to launch his new project, *In the Grip of the Lobster*. Teaching himself to edit even as he works, everything is tried and retried in an effort to achieve the combinations that will evoke the greatest amount of meaning. *Normal Love* is meant to define and reach the heights of "pasty art." What that is can sooner be gotten from studying the film than speaking of it. But briefly "pasty art" refers to what it suggests—bad art. But bad in a very special sense. It is bad and "moldy" and "pasty" because it involves all that is pitiful and miserable and lost and degraded about people. It encompasses their wretched, deceitful, inherited dreams, the abominable fantasy prisons that follow their twisted childhoods and their doomed, unrequitable groping into a dismal future. The art is pasty because this is not only the subject matter but, properly, its form and method and surface. Smith is one of the least objective artists I know. His brand of creation is convincing and overwhelming because he is so inextricably immersed in it—he is his creation in total belief down to the last terrifying nightmares that it is founded on.[11]

The *Dictionary of Contemporary American Usage* defines the word "exotic" as being "of foreign origin, not native, introduced from abroad but not yet acclimatized . . . ."[12] The etymology of the word "exotic," however, indicates first origins: from without:

> . . . the word in its common use does not mean "introduced from abroad" but suggests the glamorous . . . and romantic things the naive usually associated with "imported." The strange is colorful, rich, attractive, rare and wonderful. It is usually expensive and (perhaps therefore) slightly wicked.[13]

Add to "glamorous" and "romantic" the terms ridiculous, comic, and absurd. The combination describes Smith's films and the films made by Kenneth Anger.

An emphasis on the exotic aspects of artificiality was first and most powerfully expressed in the Baudelairean Cinema's use of decor; the filmmakers built artificial landscapes for set pieces and stressed texture and imagism. Jack Smith was partial to cardboard palm trees and Byzantine arrangements. He used the sewers of New York for his enchanted oasis in the desert of exoticism.

Kenneth Anger also decorated his film sets with a rococo clutter of memorabilia and icons (*Scorpio*); costumes of veils and sequined lace (*Inauguration*); enchanted fountains (*Eaux d'Artifice*); or moonlit leaves on a Max Reinhardt-style set (*Rabbit's Moon*). His lighting and tinting techniques transformed his sets into temples or shrines (*Inauguration*). With Warhol, exoticism was first displayed in his use of cellophane and tinfoil as background in the "talkies" filmed in his studio, The Factory, and later, in his psychedelic light and rock-music review, *The Exploding Plastic Inevitable*. Of the three filmmakers, however, it is Jack Smith who remains the most exotic in his use of images and decor. His set for a film version of *Hamlet* was an exquisitely detailed landslide of meticulously arranged New York garbage and sidewalk-leavings, street signs, dead-but-tinseled Christmas trees, pools of broken glass, wigs, jewelry and tools. Throughout this display little tableaux-like sets were arranged. There was an "enchanted" glade with wishing pool; a seven-inch high plaster birthday cake suspended over an enormous coffin; a platform stage draped with large sideshow posters of a three-breasted Gertrude and a one-breasted Ophelia. Over it all leaned a network of rickety platforms, ladders, ropes for swinging from one level to another, ramps and bridges. Strewn over the floor were skulls, dolls, and dusty roses. The Jack Smith film set was a vast mausoleum of exotic artifacts where the symbols of industrial civilization were washed up on the Coney Island shore of Jack Smith's "Lost Continent of Atlantis":

> Smith has discovered that outside the usually accepted relationship, the idealistic relationship of the creative artist and his character figure, the film-maker may charge the costume of the character figure. This is to say, the costume becomes the character and the character the costume . . . . The possibilities of this proven experiment become infinite and markedly revert to the ancient theatre. A costume replaces the actor or character figure as it glissades toward the motionless motion picture spectator.[14]

High exoticism was the inspiration for the elaborate costumes, excessive jewelry, and exaggerated headdresses which adorn the "creatures" in Kenneth Anger and Jack Smith films. This exotic costuming, along with the heavily applied glitter or sequined makeup, was also the trademark of several theatre groups which emerged in the 1960s: The Theatre of the Ridiculous, The Playhouse of the Ridiculous, The Cockettes, and the Angels of Light.

Another aspect of artificiality common to Baudelairean films was nostalgia. Nostalgia embodies a longing for another time—a time which has passed. It is dependent on the evocation of memory and, as such, is a form of time-exoticism, or artificial temporality. The emptiness of a decade, the 1950s, drove men like Ken Jacobs and Jack Smith mad with longing for another time; they rhapsodized over the visual richness of the low-budget Hollywood films of the 1930s and 1940s:

> These were light films—if we really believed that films are visual it would be possible to believe these rather pure cinema—weak technique, true, but rich imagery. They had a stilted, phony imagery that we choose to object to, but why react against that phoniness. That phoniness could be valued as rich in interest & revealing. Why do we object to not being convinced—why can't we enjoy phoniness? Why resent the patent "phoniness" of these films—because it holds a mirror to our own, possibly.[15]

Jack Smith's list of old favorites includes:

> The whole gaudy array of secret-flix, any flic we enjoyed: Judy Canova flix (I don't even remember the names), *I Walked with a Zombie, White Zombie, Hollywood Hotel,* all Montez flix, most Dorothy Lamour sarong flix, a gem called *Night Monster, Cat & the Canary, The Pirate,* Maureen O'Hara Spanish Galleon flix (all Spanish Galleon flix anyway), all Busby Berkeley flix, *Flower Thief,* all musicals that had production numbers, especially Rio de Janeiro prod. nos., all Marx Bros. flix.[16]

The Theatre of the Ridiculous

At the beginning of the 1960s, Smith and Warhol were both involved with Underground Film and off-off-Broadway theatre in New York. There was a symbiotic relationshin between the two arts, largely due to the repertory exchange of actors between film and theatre. That relationship had a major influence on the Baudelairean Cinema aesthetic.

The off-off-Broadway circuit—happenings or plays usually given in coffee house theatres (such as the Cafe La Mama)—was launched by Ronald Tavel's Theatre of the Ridiculous. Off-off-Broadway theatre's "superstars" were the same superstars of Smith and Warhol films. Tavel had worked as Warhol's scenarist throughout most of Warhol's second phase of filmmaking; his scripts were written to suit Warhol's static camera technique.

In both avant-garde film and theatre exoticism evolved as never before; the "Camp" of the 1960s began to turn in on itself and became more and more extravagant and exhibitionistic. On the west coast, the most recent survivors of the Theatre of the Ridiculous style are The Cockettes and their more radical splinter group, The Angels of Light. In his book, *People are Crazy Here* Rex Reed described The Cockettes as:

> . . . the current sensations of counter-culture show business, the darlings of the powerful underground press, a landmark in the history of new liberated theatre . . . . Mostly they are hippie drag queens, but you have to be careful with the semantics, because although the group is largely composed of men in women's clothes, it also includes women, married couples, even babies. They refer to themselves and their work as "Sexual Role Confusion" . . . . The Cockettes, named after the abominable Rockettes at Radio City Music Hall, is not a revue or an act; the only way I can describe it is a nocturnal happening composed of equal parts of Mardi Gras on Bourbon Street, Harold Prince's *Follies,* old movie musicals, the United Fruit Company, Kabuki and the Yale University show . . . .[17]

Fran Lebowitz described The Cockette's performance in New York City:

> Sequins and glitter. Perfume and glitter. Incense and glitter. Tap shoes and glitter. Old movies and new plays. Five of these plays in one week. Every waking hour another vision of peacock feathers and purple lipstick.[18]

The whole scene resembled some sort of sequin-encrusted 1966 Happening. Eventually the show started. It was a not overwhelmingly original pastiche of bits, songs and dances—"erotica and exotica" as they said on their poster.[19]

The Cockettes were not the only group to recycle old movie plots into underground theatre toward the end of the 1960s and into the 1970s in America. The Playhouse of the Ridiculous, a new development of Ridiculous Theatre, had opened at Cafe La Mama in the summer of 1972 with *Persia, a Desert Cheapie*, by John Vaccaro and Bernard Roth. It was:

. . . a parody of a Grade B desert flick . . . . [it manages] to incorporate a list of mythic/real names—Jackie Onassis, Lana Cantrell, Frankie, Dino and Sammie . . . . Film and slides are used with effective results.[20]

Stefan Brecht, writing about the Theatre of the Ridiculous, explains that "This theatre sabotages the qualities of alienation of mass culture & of the popular dream life."[21] He takes an example of mass-alienation effect from the play/film *Vinyl*. *Vinyl*, a Ridiculous Theatre piece and also a Warhol film starring poet Gerard Malanga, was a Tavel script based on Anthony Burgess's novel *A Clockwork Orange*. *Vinyl* is one of the most sophisticated and significant of the Warhol "talkies" in its exploitation of themes from popular culture. All of Warhol's "talkies," however, reflect some aspects of popular culture. Brecht explains:

The characters in *Vinyl* are out of Brando/Dean/Presley movies, the street corner gang's self-dramatizations—Doc is the sadistic, brainwashing, patient-molesting, heiress-committing psychiatrist, the charity ward brutalizer; the conflicts are out of Westerns, Eastside Kids. Chicago is the background of *Big Hotel*; science fiction paperbacks & Amazon, Queen comic books furnish the imagery of *Conquest* & (with the Bible) of *Whores* [*of Babylon*]. The themes of *Shower* are out of James Bond, popular romance stories, spy fiction.[22]

As we observed, the advent of the Underground Film stars throughout the 1960s was largely responsible for putting American avant-garde films on the pages of the *Village Voice*, and Jonas Mekas was the first to emphasize the role of the new non-actor superstar "personalities" in these films. The stylization of role-playing in Ridiculous Theatre permitted the new, personalized acting styles to evolve. Stefan Brecht describes these styles:

Though burlesque & melodrama predominate, a great variety of acting styles brings out the acting stylization. The variety emphasizes that the performers are developing their own styles according to personal relevance. Under- or perfunctory acting in a drugged state, with few, slow, set & inexpressive expressions, a blase tone (notably Ondine); flamboyant hamming in oddly slow or quick cadences, with exaggerated expressiveness— operatic melodramatic, filmstar romantic (e.g., Ludlam), expressionist, forced, pathological assertiveness (e.g., Woronow) . . . . [23]

The theme of role-playing is emphasized by the *manner* of performance. Attention is focused on role-playing as an activity of taking on a role, the actors making of themselves what they become. And the theme of role-playing is crucial *in the plays*. It is the subject of *Screen Test* and (since the Director is in the play) of *Juanita Castro*; of *Vinyl* . . . the reeducation of a victimizer into a victim; of *Shower*, in which spies (imposters) are played as movie actors (imitators) . . . . [24]

The theme of role-playing in these plays and films basically became a battle of the sexes in which the female characters emerged as conquerors. In almost all these scripts women were portrayed as vamps, movie queens, and generally as exaggerated power figures. The Theatre of the Ridiculous shared one of the most definitive characteristics of Decadence with Smith and Warhol: the emergence of the femme fatale. Describing the mythology which evolved in the Theatre of the Ridiculous, Stefan Brecht explained:

> . . . the powerful self-contained woman triumphs over a weak male locked in combat for her with other males: the male-female (mother-son, husband-wife) relationship replaced male competition at the center of things. The male has been deballed—the woman is the loner.
>   . . . the dominant figure in these plays as performed is the dominant woman . . . . Because of the plasticity of this theatre's form & style, the dominant woman need not be the same part in different productions or performances & it need not be a female part played by an actress. To dominate the action, it must be a part of some importance, acted by a strong personality, male (Ludlam, Montez) or female (Woronow, Phillips) . . . . [25]

Jack Smith and Flaming Creatures

The strong woman devouring the weak male was the theme which Jack Smith explicated through ambi-sexual, predatory "vamps" in *Flaming Creatures*. His concept of female characterization came from his deep aesthetic commitment to Maria Montez, a Hollywood actress of the 1940s known as the "queen" of the grade-B adventure films. Her influence on the formation of Smith's personal approach to film and to the creation of his creatures is evident when we read his rhapsodic description of Maria Montez:

> . . . Maria Montez Moldy Movie Queen, Shoulder pad, gold platform wedgie Siren, Determined, dreambound, Spanish, Irish, Negro?, Indian girl who went to Hollywood from the Dominican Rep. Wretch actress—pathetic as actress, why insist upon her being a an actress—why limit her. Don't slander her beautiful womanliness that took joy in her own beauty and all beauty—or whatever in her that turned plaster cornball sets to beauty. Her eye saw not just beauty but incredible, delirious, drug-like hallucinatory beauty.
>   Woman and yet imaginator / believer / child / simple pathetically believing with no defenses—a beautiful woman who could fantasy—do you know of a woman like that?
>   To admit of Maria Montez validities would be to turn on to moldiness, Glamorous Rapture, schizophrenic delight, hopeless naivete, and glitter of technicolored trash![26]

Montez is Jack Smith's exotic muse. Ronald Tavel has written that Smith, a "specialist in moldy glamour,"[27] was more influenced by Montez than any other single star. He referred to her as "the Wonderful One or The Marvelous One" and Tavel wrote of Smith:

> He felt that all the secrets of cinema lay in a careful study of the woman and this study was very influential in the formation of his personal approach to film art as well as all other arts and life in general.[28]

> Six technicolor epics followed [the triumph of *Arabian Nights* (1942)], all with the same plot pattern and slave-queen myth psychology, which earned for Universal 30 million dollars domestic in 2½ years. Their international returns are incalculable since these films continue to show widely in Asia and Africa. Most notable of the "big 6" is *Cobra Woman*, her most blatant vehicle. She played twin sisters, one good, one evil, who contended for the throne of a South Sea Island. She achieved the screen's foremost presentation of Woman-as-Evil in an orgiastic cobra dance sequence that is certainly one of the creative extremes of 20th century imagination.[29]

Thematically, Maria Montez became the Underground Salomé of the 1960s, and Tavel claims that it was his affiliation with Jack Smith during the formative years of the Theatre of the Ridiculous which resulted in Maria Montez becoming the single individual to have most influenced that theatre. Tavel described her acting as "Absolute Presence":

> She exhibited the greatest number of subtleties in her every verbal and physical gesture (meaning by subtlety that which reveals a truth about human nature) and ... she was ceaselessly interesting in every split-second that she appeared on the screen. She possessed what might be called "Absolute Presence" .... She was able, by reason of her own peculiar psychology, to embody in her single self the age-old dichotomy of good and evil, and this made her immediately suitable to project the struggle which underlies most traditional Western tales, religions, and illnesses. Because she was able, by reason of her unique imagination, to believe herself to be the fairy-tale princess, woman as the personification of evil, and finally the Eternal Woman in whom each man finds the answer to his destiny, various as the destinies of men are, she was able to embody all these roles. Also, she was beautiful; to some, the most beautiful woman of our times.[30]

Throughout the Underground theatre of the 1960s in America, there emerged another Decadent character: the androgyne. Jack Smith's androgynous creatures and the Theatre of the Ridiculous' methods of "sexual role confusion" developed the androgyne into a grotesquely potent theatrical device. Brecht remarked that:

> The drag queen is the central figure in these spectacles: not as character in the play nor in terms of plot, but by his costuming & deportment on the stage ....
> He poses not as a woman but as a man impersonating a woman.[31]

The androgynous character contributed richly to the acting style of the Theatre of the Ridiculous and the Baudelairean Cinema:

A realistic psychological androgynism prevalent in the company allows the playing of the characters not only by but as either males or females. What in conventional view would be unequivocably defeats, dominations, or inferiority may become their opposites in terms of the interpersonal psychological conflict structuring the performance.

The parts are conceived as schemata for wishfulfillment, as opportunities for will, imagination, voice & costuming: fantastic creatures, colorful, sparkling, flaming. When not romantic or glamorous, they can still be played as extreme, with a touch of the adventurous or heroic . . . . But in every play several parts are designed for strutting glory, utmost nobility, unimaginable cruelty . . . . [32]

Flaming Creatures

Something needs to be said here of Jack Smith's personal mythology. Smith's monsters epitomize "sexual role confusion;" they are androgynous characters for whom sex is, at best, a secondary characteristic. Jack Smith's personal mythology is far more complex than the thematic sexual role confusion which the Theatre of the Ridiculous used. Smith's creatures are not "humanized" personalities as are Warhol's lesbians and homosexuals. They are delicate, complicated aesthetic conceptions. In *Flaming Creatures*, they are shot so as to appear almost invisible throughout the film, we see more veils than faces, more truncated bodies than characters. The creatures are visually defined by what they are wearing and how they stand, look, move, not by a "role" of acting imposed on them but by the ways in which the camera (temporarily or partially) catches and frames them. Their insubstantiality emphasizes their mutability, their transience. Their mythical roots are entangled deep within Jack Smith's imagination. He calls our time "*The Age of the Lobster* . . . an astrological development out of *Scorpio Rising* in the Age of Aquarius . . . . "[33] Throughout his work he constantly refers to America as "the reincarnation of the Lost Continent of Atlantis."[34]

He believed, with Baudelaire, that "life swarms with innocent monsters."[35] Consequently, his pantheon of creatures includes crustaceans, mermen, sea-maidens, Ondines and reptiles. "The whole of Western culture exudes the distinctive aroma of slowly frying mermaid filleted . . . . "[36] As a director, Smith feels "more in tune with Universal, it's the only studio under Scorpio."[37] The titles of some of his pageants, performances, and slide shows were: "Travelogue of Atlantis Slideshow," "Brassieres of Atlantis," "Rehearsal for the Destruction of Atlantis," "Clammercials," "Wait for me at the Bottom of the Pool," "Lobster Moon Mixed Media Spectacle," "The Splendors that were Atlantis," "Lobster Sunset Christmas Pageant," "Bubble of Atlantis Play," "Sharkbait of Atlantis Slideshow."

In Jack Smith's imagination, the white steam out of Manhattan manholes is where the "waters are murky, exuding the marsh gases of Flatulandia."[38] Out of these vapours, rise not only the Hollywood South Sea Island Epic Princess à la Montez, but antediluvian monster-creatures as well. The following is from Smith's description of scenes in his latest film, *Normal Love* (still unfinished and not viewable as of this writing):

> . . . our lady of the Docks . . . mermaid part . . . mummy . . . corpse cutie . . . mongolian hag, cobra woman . . . mummy not cranky enough, used a werewolf instead . . . scene of the swamp with cobra woman smoking some O and dances. Indian music, CU of arms, snakes heads, mummy dragging through swamps with ruby ring . . . werewolf jumps here . . . Fish dinner used as poetic device. Most romantic invocation of woman in the world today is the smell of fried mermaid. The whole of western culture exudes the distinctive aroma of slowly frying mermaid filleted . . . . all wreaked by gooseflesh, the werewolf scampers off into the reeds with the mermaid in his arms. Heeheehee. The mango dances and sings behind them playing a miniature white violin. A hund-thou white doves are released around the cobra woman as she stands atop a magnificent sweep of stairs trying to keep the mummy from pulling her dress up. She claws his face; they struggle all the way down the stairs and teeter over the gilded brink of the moonpool, locked in a deathlove, lovehate, struggle-squirm, hammerlock embrace to the death. Why do these two creep together and quave, whooping and nibbling, breaking concentration. "Wrestle, wrestle," I yelled at them, as if in a pot-realization nightmare. Waves of fear. I yell at them, "I'm not doing retakes. Film is expensive. Look like you're fighting mad, mad at each, angry, angry, angry, no ecstasy!" The shot ends as they roll into the now bubbling and steaming moonpool.[39]

Smith's most notorious film, *Flaming Creatures*, was shot in the summer of 1962 for $100 on outdated army surplus Dupont black and white film stock. Most of the sets were constructed on the roof of the old Windsor Theatre on Grand Street in Manhattan. (The oldest standing motion picture house in New York City, the building has since been demolished.) Smith's cast was composed of actors from the Theatre of the Ridiculous: Beverly Grant, Francis Francine, Joel Markman, Mario Montez. Smith said, "The characters were my friends, and my friends the characters."[40] Smith used a non-reflex Bolex camera. The shooting took eight weekends and the editing one week. First screened at Underground Film showings sponsored or arranged by Jonas Mekas, the film's notoriety spread like wildfire and within one month of its premiere at the Grammercy Arts Theatre, was confiscated by the New York Police Department and banned by the censors.

> What was most shocking to the public and authorities was not the inclusion of exposed genitals, but the presentation of human flesh and sexuality as acceptance of the human body as if there was nothing ugly or wrong with them. The N.Y. judges found a primeval acceptance of the human body not up to community standards and banned *Creatures*.[41]

The following is a description of *Flaming Creatures* taken from notes made during numerous screenings. The script breakdown into sequences is in accord with Sontag's division of the film into seven sequences:

First Shot: Mysterious, smokey/veiled portraits glide by the title card. A blast of raspy casbah music. Secret whisperings, "Ali Baba comes today." The snake-dance music continues behind at least ten minutes of hand-drawn scroll titles, partially obscured by kissing creatures, intercut with gray, grainy pornography, studies of a flower, portraits. Crew card title is repeated three times within the end of the languid montage.

Sequence One: The white blossom-tree. Grancine Francine, matronly elegant drag queen (the Sheriff of *Lonesome Cowboys*), poses for a beautiful woman in black. Francine is all in white, both are dressed elaborately in 1920s style, hats and fans. They greet one another and wave effetely at the camera. They smile for it, for each other, then back again in absolute parody—disdain for the camera. Both look down their noses at us. A shot of the dark woman, seen through black lace, in languid reclining pose. Music comes in behind another shot of a cherry-blossom tree; "Anapola ... Pretty little flower ... " is the song on the sound track.

Sequence Two: The lipstick commercial. Francine, in MCU wearing a white silk turban, attentively outlines her mouth. Delacroix-like portraits of others doing same, looking into mirrors. One creature oblivious to a limp penis which is draped over its shoulder. Dialogue between Francine and Smith. Francine is extolling the virtues of the "new, heart-shaped limpstick (limptick?) that makes outlining your mouth as simple as signing your name."
  S: "But how do you get it off of a cock?"
  E: "No, no, you shouldn't get lipstick on your cock. This lipstick is indelible, it stays on your lips." (The shots in this scene, exquisitely composed groupings of creatures in MCU, slide into visuals of next sequence.)

Sequence Three: Chinese music. Seduction between FF and the dark lady. Series of CUs between the two, delicate nuances of pursed lips and demure glances becoming increasingly teasing and ominous. Chase: creatures running past camera, back and forth in MS, more in a parody of a chase. FF captures the dark lady and, despite fluttering protests with a fan, drags her down in front of the blossom-tree.

Sequence Four: The rape. A breast is bared in extreme CU; the dark lady is ravished by several creatures to ominous chords of electronic music. Horrible squeals and flopping struggles. Sequence builds and visual tone changes from crisp black and white to grey and white. CUs move in for more exclusively CU sequence. Finally, a shot of the dark lady-victim staggering backward and collapsing into the arms of a blond vampire-creature who drags her off. EARTHQUAKE SEQUENCE. Vibrating camera. Begins with quaking lamp.

Sequence Five: Interim: Stravinsky violin music; victim and vampire languidly reposing. Petals fall and veils and sand blow across their bodies. Very Scheherazade. End shot of victim's body now covered with piles of cloth, debris. Veil blows past the blossom-tree. Sweeter violins. Solarized greytones: ECU petal lying on ground. Silence. More violins. A fly crawls. Quiet violins and more silence. A pan down the tree, another fly in ECU. Suddenly a loud blast of honkytonk music and shot of coffin disturbs the mood. Coffin lid moves. Return in mood to fly and violins. Then violent return to coffin and vampire emerging, dancing-camping to "Honky-tonk-angel-from-the-wild-side-of-life" music. Dances with calla lilies, with FF. Echoing gongs and cacophony mixed into sound track. Long, 360°-and-more-revolving-overhead pans (10 minutes), camera dances, sees dancer from lamp's point-of-view, dances around tree. Vampire attacks victim—falls back, grimacing, satiated, lips twitching horribly; overhead shot of fall backwards then repeat of initial fall back shot in MCU, with twitching mouth. Music: Gene Vincent's "Honky-tonk Woman."

Sequence Six: MS. "Siboney." Sailor, black drummer, tiny tropical trio. Enters the fan of Montez. Cut in with CUs of other creatures dancing together, CUs of background flesh. Montez makes dancing entrance, background posing of vampire with flower, other creatures. Montez re-take entrance, same intercutting repeated, all dance after second creature entrance. Spanish marching music. All dance shots of creatures (not "Marilyn Monroe") awash with pearly-pastel sunlight. "Siboney." Wash of pale whites and greys. Intercut with dark CUs of "Marilyn Monroe." Intercuts of Delacroix poses. M.M. dances over bodies of others, twirls, rose in mouth.

Sequence Seven: Camera-caressing portraits of vampire and creatures, they pucker lips into Mick Jagger-mouths. Camera slides over sets, faces, satins. The End. Breast. All lie back. Breast, ECU.

Moreau, Anger, and Rice

Throughout this section of the paper we have examined the various ways in which the culture of the 1960s in America expressed the aesthetics of Decadence in painting (Warhol), plays (Theatre of Ridiculous), happenings (Jack Smith), and films (Smith, Warhol, Anger). While not every artist discussed here shows all the characteristics typical of Decadence as we have defined it, each of them includes one or another major theme.

In making this survey of film theatre and painting, we have indicated common characteristics in theme and content between the art of the 1960s and that of the 1890s. To continue our analogy between the works of artists in the two eras, a comparison of styles must be made. The artists, actors and scenarists of the 1960s drew heavily on social and popular themes and used the Decadent/Symbolist techniques of the nineteenth century in painting and literature. Visualizations of Decadent literary techniques (an exaggerated concern with parts over the whole: the use of glamorous, exaggerated syntax, sustained metaphors, neologisms, synaesthesia and correspondences) are evident in many of the Baudelairean films. These films also apply certain techniques adapted from Decadent/Symbolist painting: the composition which stresses parts over the whole, Mannerist distortion, expressions of the sensual, the dreamy or veiled subject, or the mythical subject (usually a "chimera" or monster) of the sort found in the paintings of Gustave Moreau.

In chapter 2 we have shown how nineteenth-century literature and the arts endeavored to satisfy the extremes of man's desires. The Symbolist painters created the ideal of "painters of the soul"[42] and this world was reflected in a dream of shadowy nuances.

The Symbolist paintings seemed to give off an atmospheric mist which veiled man's instinctual desires under a mask of strategically expressed beauty. Symbolists often used subjects which conveyed evil and eroticism as a means of expressing man's desire for ecstasy rather than a natural pleasure to be enjoyed for its physiological satisfactions. Man's hunger for infinity was expressed in the fantastic imagery—the mythological beasts—of the Symbolists. This imagery had an almost mesmeric power.

The master of Symbolist imagery and the artist considered to be the most influential of the Symbolist painters was Gustave Moreau. Philippe Jullian uses Moreau's painting *Les Chimères* (1884) to illustrate the myths, religions and preoccupations of late Romanticism and Decadence. "It presents a vision close to that of Goethe in the second part of *Faust*, and that of Flaubert in *La Tentation de Saint Antoine*."[43] This huge canvas, on which Moreau worked for twenty years (and which he never finished), is a vision of multiple chimerae languidly assuming decorative poses. It presents a baroque Symbolism and has a highly detailed, almost transparent texture. The artist seems to have interlaced fragments and groupings of chimerae, gods, monsters, angels and other religious and mythological beasts. These "creatures" appear as though part of an immense tapestry. Multiple levels of texture and edges of character-groupings are often superimposed and the composition is strikingly artificial in its emphasis on intricate and elaborate design. There is a tendency to sacrifice the whole to the details—a basic tenet of Decadence.

Writing about *Les Chimères*, Moreau described his creatures as:

... all ill-starved damned queens who have just left the Serpent. These are beings in which the soul is abolished, waiting at the side of the road for the lewd goat mounted by Luxury to adore his passage; isolated beings, somber in their dreams of desire of unsatiated pride, in their bestial isolation. Women astride Chimeras, Chimeras of Space, of Water, of the Shadow, and of the Dream.[44]

Moreau painted exotic biblical and mythical subjects, and his most famous work is probably *Salomé Dancing Before Herod*. The scene is layered with richness of texture as well as symbolic interpretation. It has enough allegorical accessories to fascinate the most repressed Victorian spirit of any generation. The total atmosphere of dark, hazy Moorish arches is filled in the foreground by filigree painting, inlaid floors, faint columns (the woman is dominating here) and gilded ornaments hanging overhead. Herod, crouched on his throne, seems small and impotent. All the nearby figures are weighted against him: Salomé's mother as an incarnation of evil, holding a peacock feather; a panther luring men and beasts with the sweetness of its breath; dead flowers strewn around while Salomé holds a fresh-cut lotus in her hand; a sphinx-like statue with a male victim under its paws; and a background statue of Diana of Ephesus, goddess of fecundity, who is judging the future fertility of mankind. It is interesting to see how Moreau changed Salomé from earlier sketches of Eastern dress (sari and African-styled headdress, plus distinctive ornate sandals) to a less Oriental costume with a domed helmet and scarf and flowing robes, encrusted with embroidery.

One other major painting by Moreau, *Le Triomphe d'Alexandre le Grand*, an 1890 oil-watercolor-tempera, is, in style if not in content, a completed version of *Les Chimères*. *Alexander* is a breathtakingly elaborate rendition of men, palaces and animals; and the picture glitters in one's mind (as does *Salomé*) long after one has turned away: Buddhas, demigods, elephants, processional corteges, and temple-thrones emerge from the collage in layers of many separate dimensions.

Alexander approaches a style of surrealist art not to be seen until well into the twentieth century (e.g., Arshile Gorky), and it represents a departure from Moreau's usual biblical/mythical foundation. The various "layers" of tableaux and processionals within the painting create mesmerizing or gravitational effects on the spectator. Moreau's work often features background pools, ominous chasms and ravines which further suggest an effect of descendance "into" the canvas.

The three Symbolist paintings by Moreau permit a technical comparison between his canvases and work of two Baudelairean filmmakers, Kenneth Anger and Ron Rice. What does Moreau's work have in common with these Baudelairean filmmakers?

Sheldon Renan has said of Ron Rice, "Possibly his vision of life was too extravagant to live."[45] Rice's film *Chumlum* (1964), made with and starring Jack Smith (and Joel Markman, Mario Montez, and Frankie Francine), is, as Renan has written:

> . . . an Arabian nights vision of a palace brothel . . . . In it gorgeously costumed characters, surrounded by diaphanous draperies, fumble through vague and erotic acts in hammocks. Much use is made of super-impositions, creating a sensual flow of color and space . . . . [46]

We can recognize almost all the "creatures" in *Chumlum* as members of Smith's cast from *Flaming Creatures*. Rice's use of superimposition was as unique to the film medium as Gustave Moreau's technique was to painting. In fact, the ten rolls of in-camera superimposition were shot at cast parties held on several occasions in the evenings after Jack had completed the days shooting on *Normal Love*, his uncompleted successor to *Flaming Creatures*. The creatures remained in costume; Jack and Ron directed and filmed their evening orgies.[47]

> The most striking thing about *Chumlum* is the combination of people and texture; of groups doing things with swinging cloth. Individuals exist as part of a whole fabric; cloth is often superimposed so flatly on people that they seem to be struggling to survive as people; as the film forces them into a larger picture, a world of painful perverse orgies and at the same time an almost spiritual vision of paradise . . . . . his frames celebrate the

beauty of textures. He does not try to cover over all the objects with a general kind of surface texture (in the very different ways that von Sternberg or Warhol do); rather he relishes the individual textures of each object, living or inanimate . . . . While it seems at first to be more on a surface level, the superimpositions do not always emerge . . . . [48]

This effect is quite different in Anger's *Inauguration*, where six crisply differentiated layers of superimposition are "at work" independently but simultaneously on the screen. Anger's superimpositions are layers of highly contrasting colors; Ron Rice's superimpositions are layers of pastel colors which retain their differentiation by each image's sharply etched focus.

Chumlum's uniqueness comes, like the painting *Alexander*, from its interdimensionality. The entire form of *Chumlum* is expressed as continuous parting-to-reveal. The whole screen is awash with Rice's curtains, hammocks, streamers of paper and ribbon, hair and feathers, swinging textures, wrapped compositions, and the movements of his swathed creatures, touching and caressing. At times, because of Rice's continuous back-winding and re-shooting technique, the movements of the same characters may be superimposed, and one sees the same character superimposed in different sizes. Characters peek through or wander into compositions, the camera traces the paths their movements leave, patterning characters into groups. There is a magic shifting from one level to the next as scenes seem to float off effortlessly or peel away. Sizes, colors, characters and movements are all taken together as a pattern of the richest visual tapestry ever achieved in the cinema. Rice and Smith seem to alternate between painting their creatures with transparent silks and drenching them in deeply colored shadows. In the dawn sequences toward the end of the film, the "exhausted" (oversuperimposed) silver halide grains on the emulsion seem to give off the "phosphorescent glow of decay."

Philippe Jullian wrote that "The Symbolists' world is reflected in a dream . . . ."[49] Gustave Moreau and Kenneth Anger were both labeled as Symbolist artists by their peers, yet they are separated by a century in time. Anger's films mix occult characters and characters from Pop culture; and the films include dreams as part of their scenario (see *Fireworks*). Similarly, Moreau merges his mythological and biblical figures in the context of many of his works. As for symbolic representations, both artists use the mythical-character method to convey "evil" and erotic messages. A cross-referencing of characters who represent allegorical ideas in Moreau's *Salomé* with those in Kenneth Anger's *Inauguration* would probably come out an obsessive tie.

The absence of light plays an important role in both artists' styles. In fact, Moreau's work often depicts a funereal gloom. Anger used opaque backgrounds in *Inauguration*, and *Fireworks*, and twilight-tinting in *Eaux d'Artifice*. Anger uses fire as a controlling factor, (albeit a malevolent one), while Moreau brings a dark glimmer to *Alexander*, a brooding glow to *Salomé* and to all his religious paintings.

Anger's discipline is lodged in a special Symbolist mythology called "Magick" which we shall examine in detail in chapter 5. Anger is so immersed in "Magick" and astrology that his work carries many more esoteric resonances than the paintings of Moreau. Anger's Decadent themes are ascending, glorifying in the verticality of composition and montage (edifying the same popular images that he critiques), while Moreau depicts a descent into a fearsome environment, haunted by biblical and mythological characters and chimerae.

4

The Influences of Surrealism and Jean Cocteau on the Baudelairean Cinema

Introduction

Before continuing our study of the critical implications of Jonas Mekas's trend-label, the Baudelairean Cinema, it is necessary to place this trend within the history of avant-garde cinema. In an attempt to situate the films of this trend within the larger body of work we will analyze surrealist and Decadent/Symbolist themes and styles in two prototypical French avant-garde films and several Baudelairean films.

In order to discover a school, a movement, or even a trend within works of major avant-garde filmmakers, it is first essential to consider their common origins. In this study the surrealists are seen to extend chronologically in both directions, bridging the concepts of Baudelaire and those of the American Baudelairean Cinema. The method applied here will be one of comparative analysis and will further enrich our definition.

As we shall observe, many of the tenets of surrealism are similar, and, at times, identical to those of Decadence/Symbolism; the spark was passed from Lautréamont and Baudelaire to André Breton. Surrealist poets and painters related directly to the Symbolists through shared specific world views and concerns. In the conclusion of his book, *Dreamers of Decadence*, Philippe Jullian examined the two movements:

> Surrealists and Symbolists had two attitudes in common, both inspired by Baudelaire: the attitude of the *poète maudit* and the desire to shock the bourgeois . . . . [1]

> . . . the cinema gave an increasingly mechanized world the images of which Symbolism had dreamt thirty years before. Surrealism, which, unlike the cinema, was addressed to an elite, thought it was carrying out a revolution when in fact, in many respects, it was simply continuing the poetic movement that began two generations earlier.[2]

We will see that some concepts of the Decadent/Symbolists were later expressed through the revolutionary vitality of surrealism and the mechanism of the cinema.

Social pessimism was a major characteristic which Decadent/Symbolists and surrealists held in common. The hatred of social order and convention of the surrealists was, however, of a more aggressive sort. Open rebellion was the surrealists' answer to their disgust with modern civilization and the oppression of its corrupt values. Their call for violent liberation from "the wear and tear of life that bites like acid into our flesh" was a call for anarchy, for "a cleaner life in the heart of the technological age that corrupts . . . . "3

The Decadents' pessimism and their hatred of the decaying values of modern life was so bitter it was debilitating. They had only enough energy with which to survive and refine their methods of criticizing civilization while still wallowing in its wane. For them, it was too late for revolution; further destruction was unnecessary with the Apocalypse already underway.

A major difference between the Decadent/Symbolists and the surrealists was the former movement's concern with the individual. The narcissism inherent in the Decadent/Symbolist perspective kept their world view on an individualistic plane while the surrealist movement involved collective as well as individual action against society; the two movements advanced different forms of rebellion and resistance. Surrealist activity was always given a social rather than strictly individual justification, while the Decadent/Symbolist theory of art for art's sake was totally divorced from any social, religious or political function. The surrealists used their arts as means to socio-political and religious ends.

Examples of surrealism are revealed clearly in Dalí/Buñuel's *Un Chien andalou* (1928). Jean Cocteau's film *Le Sang d'un Poète* (1930), made concurrently,4 contains many Decadent/Symbolist motifs. Throughout this section we shall study the influences of these two films on the Decadent/Symbolists of the 1960s avant-garde cinema: Kenneth Anger and Jack Smith. Our study will trace surrealist influences in the films *Un Chien andalou* and *Blonde Cobra*, as well as Decadent/Symbolist influences in *Le Sang d'un Poète*, *Scorpio Rising*, *Inauguration of the Pleasure Dome*, *Lucifer Rising*, and *Invocation of My Demon Brother*.

Surrealism in *Un Chien andalou* and *Blonde Cobra*

Black humor was inherent in surrealist philosophy for obvious reasons. Alfred Jarry wrote that "laughter is born out of the discovery of the contradictory."5 Surrealists saw a divorce between man and nature and abhorred the rise of the bourgeoisie for whom, "Reason, logic, categories, time, space, two-and-two-makes-four have ultimately come to seem the only living realities . . . . "6 The surrealists recognized that there was a mysterious, unfathomed aspect of human life that was being ignored, and, in fact, bankrupted, by a modern civilization. The awareness of the repressions of a hypocritic, bourgeois society was endemic to the surrealist viewpoint as they were commited to the total liberation of man and his mind. The surrealists were dedicated to the destruction of the shackles of family, morality and religion, as they believed that the dissolution of traditional human relation-ships would lead to a new type of man. However, before this new man could be reached and a new life planned, "much must be demolished, and laughter is still the best tool for loosening hypocrisy's grip."[7]

Suicide and madness were seen by the surrealists as forms of rebellion and resistance. It was a necessity for the surrealists to make a primary decision: if one was to extract him/herself from the cage of bourgeois order, it was necessary either to undergo *self-annihilation* (suicide) or to adopt the methods of *self-transformation* (through humor, madness and revolution).

The very fact that the surrealists confronted themselves with the possibility of self-annihilation as one answer to life's dilemma points to the fact that their entire search was one which was based firmly in material reality but also aspired to transcend that reality. Antonin Artaud (a one-time member of the surrealist group), in his contemplation "On Suicide" wrote:

> If I commit suicide, it will not be to destroy myself but to put myself back together again. Suicide will be for me only one means of violently reconquering myself, of brutally invading my being, of anticipating the unpredictable approaches of God. By suicide, I reintroduce my design in nature, I shall for the first time give things the shape of my will.[8]

Suicide was defended by the surrealists as a matter of principle, and was in fact, responsible for the deaths of Jacques Vaché and Rene Crevel among others.

Madness became a second tactic for rebellion. Madness, like suicide, had a special attraction for the surrealists due to the fact that those people who were labeled insane or mad, had, in one form or another, divorced themselves from the restrictions of the bourgeois order that surrounded them. The surrealists' defense of madness preceded from a specific concern with the mental process of paranoia. It was believed of the paranoid that "far from submitting to this world like most 'normal' people, he dominates it, molds it according to his desires."[9] The surrealists attempted to induce madness, invoking trances within themselves. But this, of course, was only a simulated madness, one from which they could return, more or less at will, so that they could report back on their findings. The synthesis of the real and the imaginary was extensively refined by the painter Salvador Dalí of whom it was said, "he has lived as a brother with madness and can simulate its ecstasies with much greater facility than he can imitate the so-called sane."[10]

In addition to humor, suicide and madness, dreams were used as a method for transcending the "shabbiness" of bourgeois existence. The most vital feature of surrealism was its interest in discovering that point at which the imagination sought to express itself in a more concrete form than words or plastic images. Surrealism located that point within the individual as being the dreaming state. Those following the surrealist philosophy believed the dream state to be as important an aspect of material reality as the waking state. It was from that initial assumption that the surrealist methods took root.

Indeed, dream methodology was inseparable from the original definition of surrealism. In 1924, André Breton wrote that "surrealism is based on the belief in the superior reality of certain forms of previously neglected associations, in the omnipotence of dream, in the disinterested play of thought . . . ."[11] Through the use of dreams and dream imagery, surrealist methodology sought to duplicate the automatic (unconscious) expression of the thought process itself. The surrealists essayed what they called the "experimental dream," and relied upon automatic inspiration and chance ("objective hazard").

In the late 1920s in France, it became stylish to see the motion picture as an ideal means of surrealist expression—not merely being a pictograph poem, but a moving picture poem which could resemble the dream state. Film is capable of producing an unreal, artificial experience, and in that manner, was suitable to the surrealist sensibilities. Antonin Artaud, among others, saw cinema as a machine invented specifically for translating dreams. As the avant-garde began to encounter the writings of Freud, it was almost inevitable that cinematic techniques would be seen as an ideal way of freeing images in time and space, and that the paralogic of images would no longer be subject to rational order.

Surrealists sought to liberate the cinema from conventional laws of spatial/temporal continuity through the use of dreams, stream-of-consciousness and automatism, attempting to develop forms of cinematic meta-language. By practicing psychic automatism, the artist or filmmaker became a tool for the transcription of "messages" which would surface in random order, but the randomness would be structured by the artist's and the spectator's unconscious. The surrealists rejected the conscious rational ordering of a narrative logic in their films, relying on the system of mysterious circumstances (what André Breton called "the automatic life").[12]

Early American avant-garde films of the 1940s, like the French surrealist films, could be viewed as experimental forms of psychic release. These films' images gyrated in concrete irrationality to structure a dream-like narrative.[13]

Early American avant-garde films which deal with dream-like narratives have recently been identified by P. Adams Sitney as the Psycho-dramatic Trance Film. It is important to note that Sitney selects a French surrealist film (*Un Chien andalou*) as well as Cocteau's *Le Sang d'un Poète*, to represent what he establishes as an American film trend, thus emphasizing the long-range influence which the surrealists and Cocteau had on the American avant-garde. Sitney's Trance films contained a quest for the hero-artist's identity but, as an extremely introverted mode, did not always reflect the surrealist belief that it was necessary to shock the spectator by violating his senses (*épater la bourgeoisie*)—which Luis Buñuel had described as a method: "To produce in the spectator a state which could permit the free association of ideas, it was necessary to produce a near traumatic shock . . . ."[14]

The title, "Once Upon a Time," which opens the film *Un Chien andalou* is a birth certificate for the first major surrealist film. The year was 1929 and the artists were Salvador Dalí and Luis Buñuel. One might ask in what ways the Dalí/Buñuel film was so directly related to the surrealist philosophy at the time. Stated Herbert S. Gershman in his *The Surrealist Revolution in France*:

> One can assume, therefore, that the best surrealist films would be those that bring together disparate items (or people), photograph them in unlikely (but stylized) situations, explain nothing (but do so in oracular terms), add a bit of wry humor (or horror) and break two or three of the more obvious taboos (incest, sadism, gross anticlericism, and so on).[15]

Such a post hoc description (however overly formulated it might seem in comparison to the avowed surrealist disdain for formula and structure) is, nonetheless, an accurate outline of *Chien*. In this film, disparate objects abound; in one scene, all being pulled by a pair of ropes, we have a cork, a melon, two parochial school teachers (our first obvious taboo broken) and two magnificent pianos, which are piled with the corpses of donkeys whose hooves, tails, rumps and excrement are overflowing the cases (our second taboo). Through the film we also have occasion to see two hands shaking a silver cocktail shaker in the place of a doorbell, a severed hand in a box, books turning into pistols, and so on. The unlikely and horrible situations that we are witness to also include a crowd of onlookers on a street watching a young androgyne prodding a severed hand with a stick. Wry humor is displayed by the appearance of a lady's armpit hair where a man's mouth should be, by a chaotic and mad chase sequence, and by the cyclist who falls suddenly and unflinchingly from his stopped bicycle. Horror greets us at the opening of the film with a razor blade that seems to slit open a woman's eye in tight close-up, and as an army of ants emerge from a hole in a man's mutilated hand. The young androgyne standing in the middle of the street is unhesitatingly run over by an auto.

Looking closely at the surrealist elements in *Chien*, we can see aspects of Decadent/Symbolist thought operating behind the surrealist technique. Surrealism in *Chien* is a tool for the expression of disgust with social oppression. Each sequence in *Chien* is a study of frustrated passion—disgust is expressed through the hero's rage and his impotence; violence alternates with pessimism; despite his violent struggle to survive, the hero is repeatedly (symbolically) killed or castrated; his idealism is finally conquered by pessimism. Frustration, born of repression, unleashed in the form of a violent act, is a surrealist idea, just as sterile, passive pessimism was a Decadent one.

Surrealism called for violent and passionate involvement in all forms of liberation; the Decadent's passive stance, his refusal to take part in political or religious causes, his total lack of faith, his narcissism and isolation were simply other ways of responding to the same profound disgust with social repression.

In *Chien*, we are shown frustration of love by society. The film, according to the Freudian analysis of Raymond Durgnat,[16] repeatedly emphasizes the themes of castration, impotence and phallic transference. In his analysis of the opening sequence, Durgnat interprets the eye and the razor as the male and female organs; the slashing of the eye is here interpreted as "sexuality viewed as a destructive activity"[17] (a characteristic we shall see developed in the Baudelairean Cinema). The horror of this opening sequence is equivalent to that aroused by the sadistic passages in Lautréamont's *Maldoror* (the "dead sea scrolls" of surrealism, if Breton's manifestoes are considered to be the open-ended bible of the movement). The slashing of the eye is a symbolic warning of forms of visual rape the audience can expect.

The characters in *Chien* are true Decadent types: the effeminate male, the androgyne, the femme fatale. Themes of suicide, tranvestitism (displacement of sexual identity), ennui and sterility run through each scene or fragment. For instance, a cyclist rides blankly through the streets, dressed in a frilly, feminine costume. Too exhausted to continue pedaling upright, he suddenly flops over into the gutter. As Durgnat described this fragment: " ... devoid of the energy of desire, our angel through sheer weariness falls .... "[18] The collapse of the weak effeminate man is followed by his "rescue" and "revival" by a masculinized femme fatale.

Images of death and the phallocentrism appear in a street scene. Society is represented in this scene as being a crowd so satiated with the overstimulation of the modern age, so indifferent to the little everyday horrors, that the sight of a severed hand on the street is commonplace and amusing.

A policeman places the severed hand in a box and returns it to the androgynous woman—an authority figure passing on phallic power to the sexless, castrated effete. She is joyful, holding the box, temporarily having (and being) the phallus, but before she can enjoy the revitalization, she is once again "castrated" and struck down by an automobile (a symbol of the modern age) in a hit-and-run accident.

Death and sensuality are united in the final encounter between the girl and the cyclist. Looking for him, she sees a moth. A series of dissolves brings it closer until we can clearly see the death's-head pattern it wears (recalling the Rosicrucian symbol for the death of a man's sexuality). The cyclist reappears, now under this sign of death. He puts his hand to his mouth and wipes it from his face. The woman reacts by redefining her own sex (mouth) with lipstick. In the final scene of symbolic castration the woman, in leaving the room, pauses to stick her tongue out at the man-without-a-mouth (a symbol for desire and creative power which has been taken from him; he is sterile, silenced). This symbolic gesture, reinforces his emasculation, and reasserts her possession of symbolic genitalia (the tongue). Durgnat sums up *Chien*'s negativism:

> His first, violent assault on the girl failed. His second, with the apparatus of culture failed too. His third, as a sensitive, also failed. His fourth, an aggressive display of not needing her fails, too . . . . [19]

The cyclist is an incarnation of sexuality, degraded and emasculated.

Chien expresses a powerfully Decadent pessimism, the certainty of frustration and failure caused by the overpowering strength of social repression. The theme of sexual and emotional emasculation is made more terrifying by the part which the victim so willingly plays in the process of his own destruction. For example, when the woman fights against his sexual aggression, she impresses him with his own impotence by merely threatening him with a phallic tennis racquet. His reaction is harnessed by representations of the most repressive social institutions (religion and education):

> Looking around for something with which to pursue his attack, he grabs two rope-ends, and leaps forward, only to be jerked back by the huge weight of the objects at the end of the ropes: pianos, priests, dead mules—the dead weight of his education.[20]

The film's parody of Hollywood acting styles and camerawork, its trick photography and erratic use of space/time in montage, its sense of absurdist humor and theatrical horror are all surrealist characteristics which belie the film's Decadent content and nihilistic message. We mentioned several of many Decadent themes, characters and concepts which appear in *Chien* not only to emphasize the Decadent/Symbolist heritage of the surrealists, but to compare this form of surrealism in the films of the 1920s with surrealism as it appeared in the Baudelairean films of the 1960s.

Some of these latter films (Jacobs, Smith, et al.) seem to draw on surrealist motifs of humor, madness, suicide and dreams to escape *into* the shabbiness of human existence and to violently express Baudelairean despair. "Why shave when I can't think of a reason for living?"[21] Jack Smith has said in *Blonde Cobra*. There are more similarities in the surrealism of the films of the 1920s and that of the Baudelairean Cinema: the desire to shock, the parodies of Hollywood styles, visions of horror, themes of madness and suicide. But while the surrealists consciously controlled their techniques for expressing their "paranoiac-critical" activities, often the Baudelaireans exhibited even less ordered forms of madness in their pursuits of self-transformation. For example, Smith's soundtrack to *Blonde Cobra* is chaotically autobiographical, his psychotic ramblings and laughter breaking out of control are less a performance than a series of exhibitions of hysteria (both visually and aurally). Kenneth Anger's *Fireworks* is a masochistic type of autobiographical liberation: the filmmaker-hero must deliver himself up to a sadistic, symbolic rape-beating and disemboweling, in order to attain sexual liberation.

With all of its surrealist characteristics, *Chien* is best remembered today for its powerful imagery, and its ability to horrify and shock the spectator. Another film, made thirty years later, has that same power; this is *Blonde Cobra*. Like *Chien*, it contains images of transvestitism, infantilism and sexual despair. Also, like *Chien*, *Cobra* contains many surrealist elements.

There are certain explicit similarities between the surrealism of *Chien* and that of *Blonde Cobra*. Although the latter film was shot by Bob Fleischner and edited by Ken Jacobs, the script, acting and entire conception of *Blonde Cobra* belongs to Smith. Sheldon Renan explains:

> In 1960, Bob Fleischner gave Ken Jacobs some unedited footage he had shot of Jack Smith during nine afternoons in 1959. It showed Smith and others picking their way through a life environment of complete desolation. Jacobs edited the footage, added a sound track of Smith monologues and music of the 1930s, occasionally running it over black leader. The result was the horrendous *Blonde Cobra*.[22]

The project, in its piecemeal process of realization, recalls the surrealists' group drawings—The Exquisite Corpse.

Returning to Gershman's description of surrealist film techniques, we can apply his specifications, or formulae, to *Blonde Cobra*; it brings together disparate people and items, photographs them in most unlikely situations and explains nothing at all; it is an expression of anguish and horror, made even more horrible by its technique of black humor. Smith and Jerry Simms cavort through disjointed New York loft locations. A long narrative in which the soundtrack relates only erratically to the visuals is spoken by Jack Smith. This technique is clearly a form of dream simulation and spectator involvement in true surrealist style. "Jack Smith assumes different roles (the Lonely Little Boy, Madame Nescience, Sister Dexterity) and tells their stories . . . these devices are used aggressively to rupture continuity and challenge the consciousness of the viewer . . . ."[23]

The long stream-of-consciousness ramblings of Smith's childhood recollections recall the automatic "dream mechanism" of the surrealist technique. Finally, the prolonged use of the black screen allows the viewer to "enter" the dream. The viewer is able to project him/herself into the film in much the same way the surrealists expected the spectator to enter into their films as they would a dream.

Chien continuously "breaks two or three of the more obvious taboos," including gross anti-clericalism, homosexuality and sadism. *Blonde Cobra*'s anti-clericalism is equal in vehemence to that of *Chien*. The priests being hauled unceremoniously across the floor in *Chien*, and the blasphemous commentary Jack Smith delivers on the Sadean orgies of the Mother Superior, "Madame Nescience," have the same flavor of profound sacrilege. The anti-clerical frontal assault equals in its vitriolic intensity that of the first act of Buñuel's *L'Age d'or*. Passages of the spoken text in *Cobra* specifically recall the final scene in *L'Age d'or* where Christ and his Apostles are shown staggering away, satiated from their forty-day orgy of sex and murder.

The strongest surrealist characteristic of *Cobra* is its horrifying "black humor" which depicts the shabbiness and stupidity of this world. Jonas Mekas called it "the masterpiece of the Baudelairean cinema . . . "[24] Renan explicates: "Whatever it is, *Blonde Cobra* is unparalleled in its manic humor and hopelessness."[25] *Cobra* is an epic poem designed by, for, and about the hero-poet who loudly laments his lack of control, often switching voices on the soundtrack to portray his demon/monsters within.

There is a comic lunacy (a prototypically "sick humor") in the images of Jack Smith, dressed as a grotesque transvestite baby, smashing radios and gouging holes in his costume with cigarettes. Film critic Parker Tyler described the closing scenes of *Blonde Cobra*:

> We can see the child's inevitable impulse-to-destroy that can so quickly turn into aggression . . . camp queen madness: hysterical exhibitions, falsetto ravings, infantile sadism . . . .
> All in all, his character seems to betoken a sexuality that is profoundly but philosophically dislocated . . . . [26]

Cobra is the portrayal of deranged sensibilities and behavioral excesses resulting in sadistic violence—a damnation of the sexual repressiveness of society. Like *Chien*, it cries out against the murder of sexual love. In *Chien*, the final image is of sand-trapped lovers, their corpses being eaten by insects. In *Cobra* we are given the image of a knife stuck between male buttocks as Smith's voice exclaims: "Sex is a pain in the ass. Sex IS the pain in the ass."[27] The blatant, sadistic image serves to smash the powerful taboo of homosexuality, as the slashed eye would shock the bourgeoisie into seeing. However, in context, this blunt cynicism and the sadistic image do not exactly conform to the surrealists' concepts of smashing social taboos. Just as homosexuality and androgyny had been previous themes of Decadence, the surrealists practically made heterosexuality their religion.[28] Homosexuality, it could be said, was not one of the surrealist themes. In *Cobra*, the image of the knife inserted between the buttocks of a male, accompanied by the statement on the soundtrack, implies homoeroticism on several levels: the "pain" of "sex" being the pain of anal intercourse, as well as the pain of being a homosexual in society, or even more simply, the pain of loving. Or, in Freudian terms, this last metaphor can be extended to mean the pain of loving as a form of castration, the protruding knife replacing the phallus. On the soundtrack, Smith tells us childhood tales of the sexual abasement the hero suffered at the hands of his evil mother. His retaliation to her cruelty is by burning (e.g., castrating) a little boy's penis, eroticism arrested at the point of the anal-sadistic stage.

Cocteau and Anger

The destructive nature of sexuality is also a major motif in Jean Cocteau's *Le Sang d'un Poète*. In the sequence "The Profanation of the Host," Cocteau, embodied in the part of the schoolboy victim, bleeds to death under the cruel gaze of Dargelos, his boyhood enemy/idol. The schoolboy is killed by Dargelos with a snowball, which in his hands "could become as evil as the knives of Spain."[29] The poet-schoolboy's blood (vitality) seeps from him as he lies dying in a sterile snow-covered landscape.

   The destructive sexuality of the femme fatale is yet another Decadent/Symbolist theme Cocteau explores. In one form she is a statue to whom he transfers his creative power, his sexuality in the form of a mouth (which previously lay imbedded in his palm). The statue becomes animated and encourages him to play out his own destruction—even delivering off-screen instructions on the proper use of the pistol with which he shoots himself. In a later scene, after the schoolboy is murdered, Cocteau says, "Having achieved her purpose, the woman becomes a statue once more, or in other words, an inhuman object with black gloves . . . . "[30]

   Androgyny, a major theme of the Decadents, is again revived in *Sang*, here formally introduced as the Hermaphrodite. The sign "Danger of Death" (which it wears beneath its loincloth), visually expresses the combination of death linked with sexuality. The Divine Bi-Unity (as the Hermaphrodite is also known) symbolizes total duality in non-sensual, physical and intellectual terms. This is borne out by Cocteau's design of a truncated "monster" whose body parts are a collage composed of equal portions of the male and female physiologies. The "monster" is fragmented, however, implying a lack of unity—the danger of the death of sexuality—sterility.

The personal mythology which Cocteau established in his paintings, writings and films had its roots deep in the Decadent/Symbolist garden of dreams. His characters, chimerae, settings and his preoccupation with ancient myth and ritual all recall the works of the Decadent/Symbolists.

There are certain differences between *Sang* and *Chien*. Although both films have symbolic structures operating in abstract narrative ways, in *Chien* the structure is more clearly psychological; the symbols are Freudian (wherein dream thoughts are represented symbolically in terms of simile or metaphor). This technique encourages one to emphasize the sexual interpretations. In *Sang*, however, there is a symbolic structure using Orphic, Jungian and autobiographical symbols.

Sang could be considered conventional in its attention to form and continuity. The entire film is bracketed by the author-poet's omnipresent point-of-view. Cocteau, masked except for the eyes, addresses the camera directly and announces his film. We are politely invited to watch the film by the author himself, who stands before a bank of studio lights. This immediately "historicizes" the film, lending it a personalized "authenticity". Cocteau is shown holding up a plaster hand, forecasting its function as a prop and nothing to be feared. It is important to compare this realistic (pseudo-documentary) introduction to the "realism" in *Chien*. Buñuel, immediately recognizable as the actor in the opening sequence, plays out his role as executioner of sight. There are no welcomes in *Chien*, just the threat that the spectator may expect to experience further horror, shock or worse from this cinema "engagé" called surrealism. Cocteau's introduction is somewhat more reassuring, foregoing the technique of *épater la bourgeoisie* in order to indulge his contrived poetic images.

As though to bear that out, the different points of view (identities) taken by Cocteau throughout the film are expressed in his written text, title cards, spoken phrases and recited poems. Indeed, all the voices on the soundtrack belong to him, as do the sculptures and handwritten cards (to which the poet signs his name).

A second structural element established in *Sang* is an external time frame—an artificially manipulated slow-motion collapse of a brick chimney. The film uses these shots as bookends to signal the beginning and end of *Sang*. Theoretically, the chimney crumbles down like a brick curtain throughout, but we only see it twice. This invisible "falling" becomes a structuring element, and, although invisible, it is not absent.

A third structural device is the dream sequence in which the poet acts as voyeur in a brothel-type hotel. He witnesses three acts in three sets (rooms). In between, Cocteau is careful to show the poet's pained effort to crawl (against gravity, as though in a dream) down the corridor of the Hotel des Folies-Dramatiques, passing from one keyhole to the next. The acts within each room are always separated from the voyeur-poet by locked doors. These "acts" are given further continuity by being structured into chapters or subsections within the dream, each vignette being separately described by title cards. Cocteau's voice comments on, as well as narrates, the film's chronology, which is so elaborate as to include a flashback dream sequence ending in a mock suicide, and an epilogue in the form of a plea for the reunification of war-torn Europe (the continent is represented by "four pieces of a torn, dismembered map . . . stuck on the bull's cloak with cow-dung").[31]

Because the film drew on narrative devices of the dream which could technically be expressed in the dream-like qualities of decor and tricks of photography and montage, using a radicalization of cinematic time and space, endless controversies have waged regarding the validity of *Sang* as a surrealist film. Perhaps it may better be thought of as a "trance-film" bridge between the surrealists and the Decadent/Symbolists of the Baudelairean Cinema.

In his opening speech in *The Testament of Orpheus*, Cocteau wrote:

> It is the film-maker's privilege to be able to allow a large number of people to dream the same dream together . . . for there is a considerable public interested in the world of shadows, starved for the more-real-than-reality, which one day will become the sign of our times.[32]

A critic like Ado Kyrou scorns Cocteau for creating "fantastique sans merveileux . . . . Cocteau creates 'fantastique' because for him that means facility, flight, abandonment of reality, a turning away from the major problems, and illustrations of narcissistic and homosexual themes."[33]

Frederick Brown points out that

> Cocteau's film and those of the surrealists have little more in common than their oneiric trappings. *Blood of a Poet* was not so much a labyrinth through which Cocteau walked half-asleep, as a treasure hunt in which he feigned surprise at finding objects he himself had planted.[34]

This manipulation was entirely anti-surrealist. A strong argument against *Sang*'s qualifications for the surrealist epithet is the artist's subconscious censoring of the film-as-dream; this technique, blocking or repressing the automatic "paranoiac-critical activity," constitutes a failure in surrealist methodology. As an autobiography of the poet's subconscious, *Sang* lacks any spontaneity of revelation. The meticulous structure houses four different narrative levels (the poet as young man, the poet as child, the poet dead, and the poet transformed into author). Its structure is contrived by Cocteau as a sort of theatrical/cinematic puzzle built of Chinese boxes:

> Each dream sequence is a play within a play. The first unfolds within a movie house and the second within a theatre, suggesting here, in the deepest core of his being, Cocteau viewed himself as an actor whose masks conceal other masks.[35]

In contrast to *Chien*, *Sang* carries the enigmatic stance of the artist within it. Cocteau's multiple voices and characterizations of his own highly personal and autobiographical mythology necessitated a distancing from his material, a repression of his fantasies into plot-material in order to remain faithful to his self-image.

The witty twists of artifice Cocteau placed between himself and his material, his art-nouveau epigrams in poetry and his plot structure served as strategic diversions for such an artist-as-dandy.

It was the qualities of myth and ritual, according to P. Adams Sitney, which *Sang* contributed to early American avant-garde film:

> ... *Le Sang d'un Poète* (1930), Cocteau's first film, was accused as being a parasite on the body of Surrealism. Cocteau made his films at a time when French art eschewed myth and ritual. Yet these were precisely the concerns of the American avant-garde artists who were beginning to make films in the late forties and early fifties.[36]

Preoccupations with themes and characters taken from various myths concerning death provide a direct link between the mythologies of Cocteau and the mythologies in the works of Kenneth Anger. We have seen how death and eroticism were major themes in the works of the surrealists. Georges Battaile, throughout his collected essays, *Death and Sensuality*, repeatedly claims that there is no better way to know death than to link it with some licentious image. Certainly this is evident in *Chien*, where Pierre Batcheff (playing the voyeur at the window) reacts to death with immediate lust, or when his dying hand gropes for the unknown woman's back and shoulders. In Cocteau's *Orphée*, Orphée (played by Jean Marais) becomes trapped in a game of *l'amour fou* with Death-as-a-beautiful-"Princess" (Marie Casarès), and follows her through a mirror into a timeless hell. The angels of *Orphée's* death zone are leather-gauntleted, dark-goggled motor-cyclists. The film is packed with extravagantly detailed mythology. Much of this mythology can also be seen in Kenneth Anger's *Scorpio Rising*; some is discussed here. Later in this study there is a more detailed examination of mythological systems at work in all the films of Kenneth Anger.

Death is both lover and pop-cult hero in Anger's *Scorpio*. His first appearance in the film is heralded by the rock song "My Boyfriend's Back". Death-as-skull-and-shroud crouches behind the Angel who polishes his motorcycle, then mounts and rides with him out into the night of "permanent vacation."[37] The film is practically a black mass dedicated to death, full of what Parker Tyler would label "fetish footage,"[38] and a gallery of pop heroes from the 1950s and 1960s. In discussing the American youth revolution of the 1960s, Anger admitted:

> I find not only a smouldering rebellion against the whole order of the adult world, but a desire to escape into the romanticism (and it's always romantic) of the death wish. It isn't even disguised. In a song that came out about three months ago [1963] called "The Last Kiss," something happens on the freeway and a guy's girlfriend goes through the windshield, so he pulls her back for the last bloody kiss. There's also a new attitude toward death: a sense of black humor . . . . I see the bike boys as the last romantics of this particular culture. They're the last equivalents of the riders of the range, the cowboys. The horse has become a mechanical thing.[39]

Discussing the works of Kenneth Anger and Jean Cocteau, Tony Rayns has stated:

> Cocteau's famous championship of *Fireworks* compliments the fact that Anger's film has close affinities with *Le Sang d'un Poète*. There is little direct borrowing but it's difficult to suggest two films with greater textual unity—notably in their respective openings: close-ups of the protagonist ill at ease in his environment and in front of his own reflection— *Orphée*'s tangle of life, love and death and its motorcyclist iconography obviously lead toward *Scorpio Rising*. Curiously, some of Cocteau's characters in *Sang* look quite strikingly like Shiva and Kali in *The Inauguration of the Pleasure Dome* by Kenneth Anger, and *Lucifer Rising*, if Anger can finally release it, will be his *Testament d'Orphée*.[40]

It may be important to note that the preoccupations with the hand and mouth images (as well as many other surrealist and Cocteau-esque themes and images) appear in Kenneth Anger's first major film, *Fireworks*. This film was made in 1947–48, and upon viewing it, Cocteau awarded it first prize in his Cinema Maudit Festival of 1948 and invited Anger to live and work with him in France. The images and thematic concerns of these two film poets are inextricably linked; this will be discussed in more detail later, as Anger's link with Cocteau is particularly important in emphasizing both surrealist and Symbolist concerns in Baudelairean Cinema.

In describing *Fireworks* Rayns states:

Anger's world is one of night, of astrological symbols, of the rebirth and rejuvenation of the pagan gods. Rather than probing at the beauty of surfaces . . . Anger reaches beneath them for their more universal impact. Anger is the American Cocteau. His characters, whether sailors, warlocks, phantoms, or motorcyclists, exist in a world of night . . . . like Anger's other films [*Scorpio*] is an examination of the self through myth, the subconscious and dreams. The figures exist like statues outlined against the darkness.[41]

Like Buñuel in *L'Age d'or*, Anger uses the scorpion as a symbol of self-destructive society. He expresses violently anti-Catholic sentiments and treats horror cynically. Like Cocteau, he blatantly expresses homosexual fantasies (both seriously—as in the violently sado-masochistic *Fireworks*—and satirically—as in the campy super-butch style of *Scorpio*). And like Cocteau, he deals with a highly structured personalized mythology and romantic imagery; where Cocteau drew upon figures from Greek myths, Anger's characters are derived from popular culture and the occult. *Inauguration of the Pleasure Dome* from his "Magick Lantern Cycle," is a bacchanal of mystical and occult visions designed to take the viewer on an imagistic voyage to just this side of infinity: "a simulated acid trip." More recently (1967-68), he undertook a sequel to that film, entitled *Lucifer Rising*, in which Tarot cards were to have been elaborately brought to life. But Anger can easily be seen as the artist-as-exemplary-sufferer (a role which Cocteau also played): at the first screening of *Lucifer* the entire original copy of the film was stolen by the "star", Bobby Beausoleil. Reacting in true surrealist spirit (self-annihilation), Anger immediately took out a full-page for an obituary of himself in *The Village Voice*, telegraphed his American friends to notify them of his "death," and departed for Europe. In London he made *Invocation to My Demon Brother*, which was a resourceful patching-together of the *Lucifer* out-takes with additional footage. *Invocation* has an electronic soundtrack composed by Mick Jagger and includes members of the London witchcraft coven supposedly responsible for psychically instigating the Manson "Family" murders in Los Angeles, California in 1969. The "demon brother" is played by an albino, who looks like a solarized version of Anger; and Anger himself, in utter frenzy, conducts a witches sabbath, wearing a magus costume. The film imparts a true sense of terror. The single-frame shots of Anger leading the sabbath ritual are the most frightening, as they are in extreme fast motion and he appears to be flying/skating towards us on an enormous stage surrounded by night. He flashes by like a hysterical sorcerer, brandishing a magic wand. Near the end of the film a black cat is thrown to the ground and instantly bursts into flame. Supernatural images assault the viewer in rapid succession in a manner which could make Antonin Artaud applaud.

5

Myth and Symbolism in the Work of Kenneth Anger

In this chapter, the films of Kenneth Anger will be analyzed from a Symbolist perspective. His work represents a type of film Symbolism that is uniquely analogous to the theory of correspondences basic to the Symbolist tradition. Here, as J.E. Cirlot has written:

> ... all cosmic phenomena are limited and serial and ... they appear as scales or series on separate planes ... the components of one series are linked with those of another in their essence and in their ultimate significance .... There is also a psychological basis for the theory of correspondences related to synaesthesia.[1]

Anger's techniques, his experiments with film form, can be compared to certain synaesthetic experiments which were developed by Symbolist poets such as Baudelaire or Rimbaud.

The films of Kenneth Anger lend themselves well to technical analysis because he is one of the most exacting craftsmen of the American avant-garde. His refinements in production quality enable him to perform cinematic arabesques of delicacy and complexity which often surpass the conventional cinema's far more expensive "special effects." In fact, Anger demands such technical perfection in his films (increasingly so, as his work continues), that he is often unable to complete his projects and they remain in the form of sketches or fragments. Anger's perfectionism, his attention to details of all aspects of film production, encourages us to consider him as a film "artisan." (He even restores his own prints by hand, traveling to archives in Europe as well as throughout America in order to preserve his work.) Jack Smith's techniques of "sloppiness" (moldiness, trash-art, anti-art) are totally excluded from Anger's aesthetic. Anger believes in the application of skill. His is a vision which, like Moreau's, has been achieved through the patient application of technique, and, like Moreau, he is sometimes overambitious. The most famous of Moreau's paintings, *Les Chimères*, was one which he never finished, although he reworked the figures of this canvas longer than those in any of his other works.

We have drawn many analogies between the Baudelairean-inspired French Decadence/Symbolism and the world view expressed in the films of Jack Smith and Andy Warhol. These "Baudelaireans" of the American 1960s visualized images from Decadent themes; or rather, Smith visualized Decadence and Warhol allowed it to expose itself. Anger's Decadent vision is atypical in that he is critical of the Decadent world view; he both expresses *and* manipulates it. In this way, he is more overtly critical of American society than the other Baudelairean filmmakers. Anger can be understood as a social diarist concerned with the images of the ongoing cultural revolution within the American 1960s, documenting cults, cult-figures, and personalities such as the Hell's Angels, Bobby Beausoleil, Mick Jagger, Marianne Faithfull, et al. Unlike Warhol (who often used identical material), Anger chooses to comment on this material. Yet his themes are derived from a myriad of different myths, cults and social phenomena as well. Anger's content can be understood as Decadent mainly in the context of his images, which are icons taken from a sick and dying society (*Invocation of My Demon Brother, Kustom Kar Kommandos, Scorpio Rising*). The images in *Scorpio* or *Invocation* are carefully portrayed as symbolic representations of death. In *Scorpio* objects (tools, machines) are portrayed as fetishes which act as milestones on the protagonist's one-way trip down death's highway. But these images of heroes and objects are presented to us for our judgment, not solely for our titillation. In these films heroes and objects have been carefully selected for their negative as well as seductive qualities. Anger records history as well as demythifies it.

We have also selected this body of films for analysis because of Anger's own assiduously applied system of "Magick"—a form of Symbolism in which his development of a cinema of correspondences is based on the associative tables of Aleister Crowley. Anger's experiments with the technique of parallel montage form a complementary system of correspondences to "Magick." Elaborately balanced networks of parallel montage operate within these films. We will also examine the ways in which Anger expresses his understanding and application of Eisenstein's structural principles of montage. The Symbolist system at work in Anger's montage is a realization of what Eisenstein had defined as a form of synaesthesia in the chapters "Synchronization of the Senses," and "Color and Meaning" in his book *The Film Sense*.[2] As is well known, Eisenstein's interest in Symbolism was of tremendous influence in his later work. Peter Wollen has remarked that:

> . . . the dominant strand throughout the rest of his [Eisenstein's] life was to be the investigation of "the synchronization of the senses" a return to the symbolist infatuation with Baudelaire's correspondences.[3]

It might be said that the Symbolist influences of Aleister Crowley and Sergei

Eisenstein, as combined in the works of Kenneth Anger, lead us back to Baudelaire.

Georges Sadoul wrote of Maya Deren and Kenneth Anger as the two most important names "in the development of the New American Cinema."[4] Both were forerunners of a generation of visionary filmmakers (Brakhage, Harrington, Markopoulos) who began their work in the mid-1940s. Recent critical attempts to draw parallels between the films of Deren and Anger through their mutual preoccupation with mystical ritual are misleading, however. Deren's interest in the occult as a system for depicting an interior state moved away from surrealist psycho-drama and toward a fascination with combining the elements of a given ritual in order to structure her narrative material. Influenced by classical aesthetics, she experimented with trans-temporal continuities and discontinuities found in the cinematic structure. With Deren the narrative form orders the subconscious into a design; ritual is used to impose an ideal order on the arbitrary order of art and the chaotic order of the world. The interior event is presented as a matrix out of which a pattern is made, and this pattern of ritual elements is combined to form the overall structure. Historically, it is useful to view Deren as a forerunner of the works of Alain Resnais or the experimental structuralists of today, such as Hollis Frampton, Joyce Weiland, or Michael Snow, rather than to see her work as simply a part of the "trance film" trend in the early American Underground.

Anger's use of ritual is quite different from any of the above filmmakers. His narrative model is constructed through a comparative analysis of myths, religions, and rituals and their associations external to their respective systems. His two works which give greatest evidence of this are *Inauguration of the Pleasure Dome* (1954–66) and, as examined later in this survey, *Scorpio Rising* (1964).

Deren was concerned with occultism as a classicist, interested in recombining its ritual orders within a system. Anger, a romanticist, sees occultism as a source of hermetic knowledge. For Anger, "making a movie is casting a spell." He claims "Magick" as his lifework and the "cinematograph" for his magical weapon.[5] He dubs the collection of his works "The Magick Lantern Cycle," has adopted Aleister Crowley as his guru, sees his films to be a "search for light and enlightenment," and sees Lucifer not as the devil but as "Venus—the Morning Star."[6] To date, all of his films have been evocations or invocations, attempting to conjure primal forces which, once visually released, are designed to have the effect of "casting a spell" on the audience. The Magick *in* the film is related to the Magickal effect of the film *on* the audience.

As a prestidigitator Anger somewhat parallels Méliès: a magician making transformations as well as reconstructions of reality. As a Symbolist operating within the idealist tradition he has a turn-of-the-century fascination with ideal artificiality: in *Lucifer* he causes certain landscapes to reveal themselves at their most magical by both capturing the moment and capitalizing on it, showing a rare moment of nature, albeit enhanced through technical effects (such as the hand-tinting and the spellbinding "star machine" which was built at the Chicago Art Institute to play red and green pentagrams over the screen and audience at his most recent presentation of *Lucifer*). Not a surrealist who puts blind faith in his own dream images and trusts his dreams to convey an uncommon unconscious, Anger works predominantly in archetypal symbols. As the magus, he is the juggler of these symbols, just as in the Tarot, where the Magician is represented by the Juggler and is given the attribution of Mercury, the messenger.

As a visionary, Anger creates his own frame of reference which is an extension of the vision and teachings of Aleister Crowley. Crowley has been called the "Oscar Wilde of Magic" and has called himself "The Beast 666."[7] An English magus born in 1875, he was a contemporary and enemy of both Freud and Yeats. He quarreled with the latter over leadership in the Hermetic Order of The Golden Dawn. Although he claimed, in criticizing Freud, "I cannot do evil that good may come. I abhor Jesuitry. I would rather lose than win by stratagem,"[8] he is reputed to have jumped official rank in The Order, illegitimately claiming the title of Ipsissimus:

> There was yet another order within the Great White Brotherhood, the top order; it bore the name of the Silver Star . . . (*Astrum Argentinium*). This contained the three exalted grades—Master of the Temple, Magus, and Ipsissimus . . . . they were on the other side of the Abyss.[9]

Entering into this ultimate enlightenment as Master of the Temple and exiting as self-ordained god, Crowley and his discovery of supreme apotheosis of the self produced his "do as thou wilt" philosophy. In his *Book of the Law* (the means by which he bridged the Abyss to Masterhood) he proclaimed: "Bind Nothing. Let there be no difference made between any one thing and another . . . . The word of Sin is Restriction . . . there is no law beyond 'Do What Thou Wilt'."[10]

Crowley's self-deification is reflected in the "joyful humanism" of the Age of Horus or the Aquarian Age. The Cosmology of his *Book of the Law* introduces the Third Aeon: after Isis's aeon of matriarchy and Osiris's aeon of patriarchy follows the aeon of Horus, the Child or true self independent of priests or gods. In his *777—Book of Correspondences*, Crowley cross-indexes Greek, Egyptian, and Hindu mythologies. Venus is found in Isis and corresponding goddesses. Lucifer is the Roman name for the planet Venus which was worshipped both as Aurora (the morning star) and Vesper (the evening star). Until these myths were suppressed by the Catholic Church the

Gnostics worshipped Aurora/Lucifer as the Herald of the Dawn, the light preceding the sun. The Crowleyan/Anger doctrine exchanges Lucifer with Horus as well: "It all began with a child playing with a chemistry set that exploded," Anger has explained, "an innocent, pure child prodigy, creating for the joy of it, just as Lucifer created his own light shows in heaven . . . . Eventually he was expelled for playing the stereo too loud."[11]

Like Cervante's *mas bello que Dios*, Lucifer's sins lie in out-doing God. He is seen not as a leader but as the totally independent, original rebel; the Luciferean spirit manifests itself in the spirit of the artist, not as a Hell's Angel. "He is also Puck [the name of Anger's production company], the spirit of mischief, mortals are the toys in his playpen, the world belongs to Lucifer."[12]

But Crowley's major contribution to Anger's vision was his invention of "Magick," the performance of ritual which seeks to invoke the Holy Guardian Angel (the aspirant's higher self), an idea adapted from the medieval magus Abra-Melin.[13] The method of invocation relies on talismanic magic: the vitalization of talismans. Originally these were drawn vellum patterns, sort of a shadowgraph print of the demon one sought to "capture."

Anger equates this with the photograph's ability to steal the soul of the subject. Medieval talismanic signatures were considered to be autographs by demons and Anger refers to them as "printed circuits" between physical and spiritual (or alternative) reality. He sees glyphs, hieroglyphs, sigils, pictographs, billboards, and especially tattoos as "magickal marks on the wall."[14] In *Lucifer* he uses the Abra-Melin "Keys" or trademarks of the basic elements as overlaid inscriptions which interact with the visual energies of earth, air, fire, and water so that the symbols "call forth" variations in their visual counterparts. "Magickal" insignias are an integral system at work in all of Anger's films. They are duly consecrated by optical isolation through special effects: the triangular "trademark" matted into a shot of Isis in *Lucifer*, the mirrored superimposition of magickal tattoos on Anger's arms in *Invocation to My Demon Brother* (1969), a door within Crowley's face which opens into a superimposed zodiac in *Inauguration of the Pleasure Dome*, the hand-tinted chartreuse fan ("the magickal weapon") in the otherwise blue-toned *Eaux d'Artifice* (1953), and, most recently the addition of hand-tinting in *Lucifer* which unites the flying falcon-of-Horus and the live Kephra scarab with their carved hieroglyphs.

To conjure a successful transformation Anger-as-Magus-Artist mixes his palette according to Crowley's color system from the Golden Dawn (a Rosicrucian order): a codified alchemical scale wherein planets are related to colors, sacred alphabets, drugs, perfumes, jewels, plants, magical weapons, the elements, the Tarot, etc., etc. In the Royal Color Tables of *777—The*

Book of Correspondences the "princess Scale" denotes the "pure, pastel colors of idealism."[15] This is the scale which Anger applies to his brief-but-beautiful *Kustom Kar Kommandos* (1965). In *KKK* he makes his invocation through the use of color, attempting the transposition of the sign of Cancer (seashell blue and pink) onto the Machine. The pastels of reflected flesh and the hard gleam of the dream buggy, from the knight on the hood to the tires, are edited together to resemble the languid movements of a boa constrictor. Dedicated to the Charioteer of the Tarot, the "dream lover" owner of the car, is Anger's "silver knight in shining armor."[16] Like the car, he is a machine built for transmitting energy; the blond boy is seated in a mirrored chamber with velvet seats designed to resemble a vulva or giant twin lips, forming a red plush vertical smile. Anger feels that *KKK* closely resembles Dalí's painting *Mae West's Living Room* in the portrayal of a maternal universe wherein power is a poetic extension of personality, "an accessible means of wish-fulfillment." The lyrics "I want a dream lover so I don't have to dream alone . . . "[17] enrich the romanticism within the phallo-centric vision of narcissistic-identification-as-virility. A dream lover is a double, a "demon brother" and a mirror-reflection; *KKK* is an invocation of the ideal, not human elements, and is dedicated to an idealization of reality.

Romantic idealization, poetic irony, lush exoticism, and the evolution of anti-classicist montage wherein the whole is subordinate to the parts all reflect Anger's affinity with fin de siècle French literature. (In 1951 he attempted to film Lautréamont's *Les Chants de Maldoror* [1869].)[18] His most profuse use of Decadent/Symbolist imagery occurs in *Inauguration of the Pleasure Dome*. However, the development of a montage-syntax that closely resembles the elaborate syntactical constructions of Huysmans and the ambiguities of Ducassian mixed metaphor[19] are nowhere more evident than in *Scorpio Rising*.

Scorpio Rising is an extension of self-gratification into self-immolation. The Machine (now a motorcycle) is totemized into a tool for power; the "charioteer" is Death (the ultimate "dream lover" by romantic standards). Violence replaces the poetic extension of personality and violent eroticism is combined with the tragic death of the highway hero ("the last cowboys"): "*Scorpio Rising* is a machine and Kenneth Anger keeps his spark plug burning on AC (Aleister Crowley) current . . . . Guess which one I was in love with ten years ago? . . . Was it the chromium or was it the guy?"[20]

Sado-masochism, death and sensuality, sex and angst—*Scorpio* is America's buried collective adolescence manifested in the isolated pop-art visions of decayed dreams. It reflects the last gasp of the dying Age of Pisces (Christianity) as a motorcycle race roaring toward oblivion. The big butch bikers encase themselves in leather; slung with chains they move indolently, like huge cats. Scorpio and his brothers/lovers ("Taurus" and "Leo"—both ruled by Venus) worship their machines. But people as well as objects denote fetishism, are transformed through mass adulation into becoming idols. James Dean is shown as the Aquarian Rebel Son; Brando, Christ, Hitler— all are objects of worship, "humans idolized by idiots . . . . The different degree of impact each had was dependent on the degree of advertising between pop stars and Christ."[21] A grade-C Christ film, *The Road to Jerusalem*, produced by Family Films, was delivered to Anger's doorstep by mistake while he was in the process of editing *Scorpio Rising*; he accepted it as "a gift from the gods," toned it blue and intercut it (as the second major montage element within the film) with the bikers' Halloween party. Christ is introduced walking with his disciples on Palm Sunday, two of the "theme songs" ("I Will Follow Him" and "He's a Rebel") link the Christ scenes to Brando and Dean; "Torture" (Gene McDaniels) and "Wipeout" (The Surfaris) link Him to the bikers' initiation and Hitler. The purpose of "following Him" is to race after the trophy, dying to be first, just as the sperm is racing toward oblivion in its desperate need to unite with the egg. The "egg" may well be the new aeon and the longed-for oblivion: the destruction necessitated by change. The new aeon is reached by moving from *Scorpio*'s "night" toward *Lucifer*'s "dawn." The skull-and-crossbones fluttering in superimposition over the cycle rally signifies the death of sensuality in much the same way as the death's head on the Masonic or Rosicrucian flags represents the philosophical death of man's sensuous personality—a transition considered essential in the process of liberating man's spiritual nature. The final shot of the film is the dead Scorpio's outstretched arm, lit by the red strobe of a patrol car, on it the tattoo "Blessed, Blessed Oblivion."

Anger's myths address mass erotic-consciousness through a barrage of notorious symbols. These often war with one another in Reichian power-trips of rape, will power, fascism, and revolution. "I find ridiculous the idea of anyone being the leader," Anger has said.[22] Pentagrams war with swastikas in *Invocation to my Demon Brother*. Brando tortures Christ in *Scorpio*; Shiva asserts absolute power over his guests in *Pleasure Dome*. Historical heroes are reduced to pop-idols and history is demythified by comic book codes. ("When earths collide, gods die.").

Considering that Anger takes an anti-nostalgia stance and deplores the fact that "yesterday's heroes are still with us" (Brando), it is ironic that at the time *Scorpio* was released it enjoyed popularity as a dirty Halloween party or as a celebration of the contemporary decadence it displayed. But today the pop *Liebestod* lyrics of the sixties ("He's a rebel and he'll never be free . . . ," or "I still can see blue velvet through my tears") have strong nostalgic resonances. Revived in the vacuous seventies, these lyrics have audiences stomping and clapping to the very songs which originally served as a criticism of idolatry and romanticism "turned in on itself and beginning to rot." The value of Anger's strategic use of pop songs transcends their being "structural units within a collage film";[23] they often act as a complicated running commentary in lyric form, performing a narrative as well as structural function. In *Rabbit's Moon, Puce Moment,* and *Kustom Kar Kommandos* the result is that the naive poetry of the song replaces the temporality of spoken dialogue in a timeless, mythic way. In *Rabbit's Moon* the lyrics "There's a Moon out Tonight" and "I only have Eyes for You" underscore the futility of "reaching for the moon"—a message visually expressed in the repetition of shots of a *commedia*-style Pierrot supplicating a Méliès-style moon which remains just out of reach. *Puce Moment* takes on a spicier meaning when the songs "I'm a Hermit" and "Leaving My Old Life Behind" on the sound track are combined with the visuals of shimmering antique dresses and a languishing Hollywood star. The obvious suggestion here is a renunciation of drag-dressing, an escape from the fetishization of costume and a climb "out of the closet." Anger's most complex and intriguing use of music occurs in *Eaux d'Artifice,* where light, color, movement, and textures are combined in baroque counterpoint with Vivaldi. With *Invocation* and *Lucifer* he has begun to move toward an exclusive use of original musical scores.

Transubstantiation is one of Anger's favorite themes. Frequently this takes the form of a reverse Eucharist where essence is converted into substance; this process can be discovered in *Fireworks* (1947—his first major film), *Puce Moment, Rabbit's Moon, Scorpio,* and now *Lucifer.* These films summon personifications of forces and spirits whose dynamic powers appear to "break through" and turn against the character and/or structure. *Scorpio*'s iconoclasm is effected by the critique which the film conducts on itself, demythifying the very myths it propounds by interchanging them with one another and integrating them into a metamyth. Christ/Satan (religion), Brando/Dean (popular culture), and Hitler (political history) are reduced to sets of systems which destroy one another through an internarrative "montage-of-attraction".[24] Thus, the film itself is the metamyth of the films which constitute it. Different dogmas are equalized (and subsumed by) their structural and ideological parallels. *Scorpio*'s auto-destruction stems from the center, "core" invocation and triumph of Satan over Christ, Machine over Man, and Death over Life.

A somewhat less nihilistic subsumation of substance by essence is the conventional Eucharist ritual performed in *Inauguration of The Pleasure Dome* and *Eaux d'Artifice.* In the former, Lord Shiva transforms his guests into spirits of pure energy which he absorbs and recycles into a frenzied, operatic orgy. The pyrotechnics of this celebration build to such visual intensity that *Pleasure Dome* "destroys" itself by growing too large for the very confines of the screen. In the original (pre-Sacred Mushroom Edition—

1958) the screen grew "wings" (like Abel Gance's Triptych) and, for the final twenty minutes, each panel of the triptych was loaded with up to six simultaneous surfaces of super-imposition (eighteen separate planes). The visual material seeks to transform itself into pure energy. In *Eaux d'Artifice*

> . . . The Lady enters the "nitetime labyrinth of cascades, balustrades, grottoes, and fountains", and tries to lure out the monsters with her fan; she's trying to invoke the water gods . . . . She fails, being weak and frivolous, and melts into the water (surrenders her identity) so that she can play on."[25]

Eaux turns its hermaphrodite hero(ine) into a waterfall. Nature wins over artifice. Human confusion is subsumed by the larger order of things.

After thoroughly examining the myths, themes and techniques in Anger's work, we are prepared to examine, in detail, his experiments with montage. Because the most advanced and complex editing techniques appear in *Scorpio Rising*, it will serve as a model.

We have seen how *Scorpio Rising* portrays the fall of an age, a revolution in culture. The catalysts for this change are black-leathered motorcyclists who exist outside and in defiance of the prevailing culture. This self-imposed, romantic alienation and violent defiance give the cyclists a place in American mythology similar to cowboys and gangsters. Anger plays on these national myths and pits them against the myths and symbols (political, religious, and pop-cultural) of the dying age, to their mutual destruction. To achieve this, Anger utilizes Eisenstein's theories of montage and conflict. The concept of intellectual montage which Eisenstein conceived and with which he experimented, is mastered and forcefully executed by Anger in *Scorpio Rising*. Tony Rayns observes that

> Anger has an amazing instinctive grasp of all the elements of film-making; his films actively work out much of Eisenstein's theoretical writing about the cinema. For instance, Eisenstein's ideal of *chromophonic* (colour/sound) montage, described in *The Film Sense*, is startlingly achieved in the "party lights" sequence [in the "Walpurgis Party"] in *Scorpio Rising*, where the Randells' hard, dense arrangement of the song—for the first time in the movie, cutting in before the end of the preceding song—is matched by a thickening in the terms of reference in the montage, while at the same time lyrics relate explicitly to the film's development of its colour scale . . . . it comes nearer [to Eisenstein's theories] than anything in commercial cinema, and produces film-making as rich in resonance as anything of Eisenstein's own.[26]

Scorpio has the form of a ritual from its beginning, in preparation, to its end, in death. The cyclic nature of the ritual suggests a timeless repetition. The film has been divided into four parts for the ritual. The "boys" meticulously preen their mechanical egos (cycles), in custom colors and high gloss chrome, and themselves, in bulging denim and leather. In "Image

Maker" (Part II), Scorpio, the film's hero is introduced. Through him, Anger probes the contents of the myth of motorcyclists. The interactions of the image and the person, each being a manifestation of the other are explored through the character Scorpio by contrast with other cultural heroes (James Dean, Marlon Brando, Jesus Christ). The end of the "Image Maker" sequence is marked by Scorpio snorting cocaine, which also signifies the beginning of the rite which Scorpio directs. The rhythm of the film begins to grow orgasmically until the cyclist's death in the end ("Blessed, Blessed Oblivion"). The "Walpurgis Party" is like a tribal rite or ceremony, a war dance to build the bikers to the proper emotional-psychological state for the execution of the ritual. The antics of the bikers at the Walpurgis Party are very erotic, in a very adolescent way. Scorpio leaves the party to inspect and desecrate a church. From the church (at night) Scorpio's demonic possession grows until he is in control of the parallel action which he directs from the altar. The montage and the action grow more and more frantic as Scorpio "oversees" the motorcycle race (day), the objective of which is not victory but death (completion of the ritual). It is the death of the cyclist which ends the rite and the film. Eisenstein wrote that

> It is art's task to make manifest the contradictions of Being. To form equitable views by stirring up contradictions within the spectator's mind, and to forge accurate intellectual concepts from the dynamic clash of opposing passions.[27]

The importance of Anger's use of Eisensteinian principle is that it is not reduced to a craft, a trick in time, but maintained as an artistic vision. In montage reality is smashed. Art comes from the filmmaker's reassembling of the splinters of time and space with the inclusion of the intellectual, psychological, or emotional content of the event. The collision of two separate images creates a third distinct impression to the viewer. Similarly the blending of two dissimilar images into one accumulative essence yields a poetically metaphoric statement on that which is portrayed. This is the artistic importance of Eisenstein's theory. Its potential is rarely realized in film, and even more rarely as true to theory as in Anger's film.

As one begins to break down the elements of montage contained within the film, it is important to remember what Eisenstein said regarding the interaction of montage sequences.

> ... methods of montage ... become montage constructions proper when they enter into relationship of conflict with each other .... within a scheme of mutual relations, echoing and conflicting with one another, they move to a more and more strongly defined type of montage, each one organically growing from the other.[28]

When one is examining Anger's use of montage, there are often several levels which must be considered. The montage can seldom be labeled as one specific method without further consideration. For instance, in a montage sequence early in the film, the visual rhythm is created through the song "Wind Up Doll." The song is begun simultaneously with shots of men tightening bolts, or other such action between men and cycles that involves a circular tightening motion. Intercut with these are shots of a young boy playing with a wind-up motorcycle. Rhythmically the montage sequences are perfectly matched. It is as though the men working on their cycles are winding up the child's toy which is run toward the camera with the child's face in the background. The rhythm established by the song is carried through the montage of the sequences. However, in the conflict of the two images there exists an intellectual montage. The fascination and absorption of the child and man are synonymous. Anger calls it "masculine fascination with the Thing that goes . . . from toy to terror."[29] The combination of images here gives both a childish innocence and adult ignorance of the consequences of actions to the action of the man. The innocence of the childish fascination is transferred from the child to the men to the extent that the motorcycle seems like a toy. At the same time there is the implication that the power that is building, through the winding and tightening will be released for the thrill of movement. The power will be released unhampered by reason, a pure experience, like that of a child.

Anger's use of music for the sound track serves a much more vital purpose than merely the creation of rhythm. The thirteen pop tunes which Anger has selected from early sixties rock and roll serve not only as a means of organization but also as an ironic narrative. The songs create conflict, on another level, with the images of the film and in this way become an essential part of the film's montage. For example, Anger creates a sexual as well as textural ambiguity through the use of the song "Blue Velvet" combined with montage in which the men dress themselves. The romance of "Blue Velvet" ("She wore blue velvet / and I still can see blue velvet through my tears") on the one hand is in ironic conflict with the very butch masculine men ("she") as they vainly, ceremoniously clothe themselves in tight blue denim ("blue velvet") and black leather with chains. On the other hand, the contents of this sequence are highly eroticized. There are many shots of semi-naked men, muscular chests and stomachs curtained on either side by a black leather jacket. All the eroticism in *Scorpio*, from the adolescent pranks of the Walpurgis Party to the explicit connotations of the sequences now in question, are homo-erotically directed. In one portion of this same sequence a man clothed only in long underwear rises up quickly from the bed into the camera, a full head-on close-up. This shot, in a montage of attractions, is followed by one of a crotch as the man zips up his zipper. The synthesis clearly implies fellatio. Elsewhere, in the Walpurgis Party sequence, this effect is repeated.

Similar to Anger's use of sound to heighten the effect of montage is his use of color to that same end. The bulk of *Scorpio* was filmed by Anger in color. Two of the major elements of montage, however, are footage from existing films. The bluish footage of Brando, shot off of television, is from the film *The Wild One* (1954). The footage of Christ was also taken from a black and white film which Anger toned blue. Before discussing the significance of color to montage, let us first examine the sequence in question.

The sequence opens with an ironic intellectual montage which incorporates the misunderstood rebelliousness of adolescence into the character, Scorpio. Scorpio is introduced with the song "Devil in Disguise." ("Looks like an angel but I got wise. / You're a devil in disguise.") He is lying on his bed in his room, reading the comics. His walls are cluttered with pictures of motorcycles, James Dean, slogans, etc. The montage forms a relationship between Scorpio, the comics and the things in his room, creating an essence of his personality which is one of the biological fury of adolescence.

At this point, a parallel montage of attraction fuses Brando (the image), who appears on Scorpio's television in the film *The Wild One*, and Scorpio (the person) into one personality. Sitney says of this usage

> It [the television] functions as an aesthetic reactor. Whatever we glimpse on it is always a metaphor for what is happening within the hero of the film. Its metaphoric level extends simultaneously as an aesthetic dimension of Scorpio's thought and action in the realm of plastic illusion and as an icon of contemporary life—the source as well as the reflection of the unconscious.[30]

As Scorpio goes through the action of this sequence, there is a constant interplay between the image qualities of Brando and the reality of Scorpio. Brando smokes, Scorpio smokes; but Scorpio burns his mouth when he tries to light the match on his teeth. When Scorpio dresses (this section is also intercut with footage of men riding motorcycles, real men, not images, filmed in color, not black and white), as he puts on his leather jacket, Brando turns, revealing the skull on the back of his. Scorpio snorts cocaine, Brando closes his eyes and grins inwardly. But the conflict ends between man and image, the image of Brando leaves the screen, while Scorpio goes out to raise hell. In fact, the image of Brando is replaced on the screen with a Hebrew menorah and a crucifix, the objects against which Scorpio's violence will be directed.

In the following section of this sequence, Anger creates an overtonal parallel in the montage between Scorpio and Christ. I refer to the montage here as overtonal because while the actions of Christ and Scorpio are parallel in structure, they conflict greatly in motivation; in fact they represent extreme opposites. In this instance the montage is overtonal because of the contradiction inherent in the associations made by the juxtaposition of the shots. The conflict exists between the structure, a parallel montage of attraction (the structure is further aided by the antithetical lyrics of the song "He's a Rebel" which apply equally to Scorpio and Christ), and the content, an overtone to the structure of the section. For example the parallel is introduced as Scorpio leaves his room and walks down the dark street. Christ walks down a street crowded with beggars and cripples. As Christ passes a beggar, there is a cut to Scorpio kicking the grid of his motorcycle. As Christ heals a blind man by touching his eyes, there is a cut to Scorpio touching the throttle of his cycle. As the blind man kneels in gratitude before Christ, there is a four-frame cut to an erect penis that Scorpio would offer him. The parallel is continued through the Walpurgis Party sequence which is contrasted with a gathering of Christ and his disciples. The relationship between the shots are direct, forming a montage of attraction.

The influence of color on this montage sequence adds yet another dimension. The conflict of color between the sequences of Christ and Brando (both in bluish-toned black and white) and the bulk of *Scorpio* (in color) creates a clear distinction between the mythic qualities of the former and the realism of the latter. Certainly there is an intimate interplay, a give and take between the two, but essentially Anger's goal is to destroy both of these myths. The toning blue of the black and white sequences further adds a sense of romantic longing for the myths and their fading heroes. These are in brutal conflict with the montage of Scorpio and the use of the hard, harsh color in those sequences. The blue-toned black and white of Brando and Christ coupled with the C-grade production values of *The Road to Jerusalem* also makes those sequences seem artificial. So the color conflict adds an intellectual slant to the montage of this sequence. Even as the associations are made, one is aware of the artificiality, the invalidity of the Christian and Hollywood myths in contrast to Scorpio and his ritual. The contrast is greatly heightened by the use of color. Anger has said of this sort of creation "I also regard the inception of new concepts and viewpoints in the conflict between customary conception and particular representation as dynamic—as a dynamization of the 'traditional view' into a new one."[31]

As we have said before, Eisenstein's principles of montage are an artistic view of reality. We have come to see montage used as a craft, to compress time, or evoke tension. Anger's practice primarily revitalizes the technique of montage and brings in sound and color in a complementary way. It is interesting that it is a cultural revolution in *Scorpio Rising* which utilizes montage in contrast to Eisenstein's political revolutions in *Potemkin* [1925] and *October* [1927]. Tony Rayns reports that

> Fascinatingly, Anger plans to use another of Eisenstein's theories in making *Lucifer Rising*; he wants to explore the possibilities of vertical composition. In his crucial essay *The Dynamic Square* Eisenstein complains that the advent of cinemascope cripples yet

further the adventurous film-maker's chances of breaking away from the limitations of passive horizontal composition: "It is my purpose to defend the cause of the 50% of compositional possibilities which have been banished from the light of the screen. It is my desire to chant the hymn of the male, the strong, the virile, active, vertical composition! I am not anxious to enter into the dark phallic and sexual ancestry of the vertical shape as a symbol of growth, strength or power . . . . " Naturally enough, this precisely *is* Anger's desire: "I guess my whole trip is phallic worship . . . . "[32]

Before examining the differences in montage technique between *Scorpio Rising* and Anger's latest work it is necessary to describe its visual content. The title, *L-U-C-I-F-E-R R-I-S-I-N-G*, rises in vibrating fiery letters from the waves of the ocean. Throughout *Lucifer* neon calligraphy and animated symbols flash, sometimes simultaneously matted onto the landscapes of ancient Egypt. Often these electrified talismans break into the material like signals from lost civilizations: picture-writing erupting through layers of history. *Lucifer*'s universe is populated with signaling gods and alchemical symbols. The work, at this stage, is largely concerned with communication between Isis (Myriam Gibril) and Osiris (Donald Cammell) through the forces of nature; this communion of natural elements provokes meteorological reactions in preparation for Lucifer's arrival: lightning issues forth from the staffs and emblems of these radiant deities; nature replies with rosy dawns, whirlpools, and emissions of molten rock. The sun goes into eclipse. Intercut with an endless torchlight procession, Lilith (Marianne Faithfull) climbs the prehistoric stairway to a Celtic shrine where, as a goddess of the moon, she supplicates the sun. The sun rises directly in the center of the solstice altar; its rays part to reveal a scarlet demon within the round hole of the rock: the blazing astrological symbol of Mercury (god of communication and ruler of magicians) appears. A magus (Kenneth Anger) stalks around his incandescent magic circle in invocation to the Bringer of Light (cf. Murnau's *Faust.*) Outside the smoking circle a Balinese fire demon (symbol of sacrifice) materializes. The magus bows before the idol, a globe of phosphorescent lightning shudders across the screen and Lucifer resplendent in satin L-U-C-I-F-E-R jockey jacket, arises from within the circle. In response, nature throws a celebration of volcanic eruptions and avalanches of snow and, ultimately, an electrical storm over Stonehenge. Isis and Osiris, the happy parents (of Lucifer-as-Horus) stride through the colonnade at Karnak to greet their offspring, and a feldspar-colored saucer sails at us from behind the stone head of Ramses II.

So ends the first third of Anger's first feature, *Lucifer Rising*. This work-in-progress is a remake and continuation of the sabotaged "Love Vision" of *Lucifer* which he began seven years ago in San Francisco. The original was to have been about today's new tribes of teenagers, turned-on children—teeny-boppers and adolescent hippies and featured a set of living

Tarot tableaux. Today's version of *Lucifer* is as much a departure from its predecessor as it is from the major body of Anger's work. But his previous works can still be understood as pointing the way to this grander, more expansive vision which is less demonic, more divine.

Lucifer Rising attempts to transcend the passive-active dialectics of power and the sexual preoccupations of adolescence, the blue of eternal longing. Its theme (so far) is that of man's reunion with his lost gods: the dawning of a new morality. The cult of arrested adolescence is replaced by the fulfillment of its longing: reaffirmation of identity through spiritual communion between man, gods and nature. Fantasy and reality are no longer distinguished but are parts of a larger, more complete universe. Black Magick goes White; the hero is the "bringer of light," Lucifer, portrayed as a demon of great beauty. This "fire-light-trip" begins with the first frames of *Fireworks* (1947) (an invocation to Thor) when a firebrand is extinguished in water. At the film's outrageous finale a sailor's penis is lit and explodes as a roman candle; this is followed by a denouement where a wax candle atop a Christmas tree dips into a fireplace, igniting the scattered stills from the film's opening dream sequence. *Invocation* (resuscitated from the leftover out-takes of the original *Lucifer*, "A fragment made in fury . . . the last blast of Haight consciousness")[33] opens with an albino demon brother kissing a glass wand; later Mick Jagger's black cat goes up in flames and the film culminates with Bobby Beausoleil short-circuiting into Lucifer. Anger calls *Invocation* a "burn."

There is more light and less fire in *Lucifer Rising* (what the neo-Platonists would refer to as the "spiritual lux"). Assertion of will has matured into communication between anthropomorphic gods; glamorous Egyptian deities within a universe which is established by an uncreated pre-condition for order—pagan spirits at play in a universe where God does not yet exist. These man-gods exist organically, as part of nature; they grow out of the shadow of cliffs and temples like living sculptures. We first see Isis as long legs disembodied by stone shadows. Isis and Osiris, glistening with health and confidence, authentically costumed, perform their nearly static ritual from the cliffs overlooking a space-like sea (Crowley's "vast abyss between man and god"). Where it was the nature of the stone water gods to overwhelm man in *Eaux*, the "new" gods in *Lucifer* embody the "best" in man: pure, free forces, calling on nature to aid mankind, summoning the elements in preparation for the Second Coming.

Lucifer is also a radical departure in visual form from Anger's previous works. No longer does the power of any given image depend on the ritualistic repetition and recombination which essentially shapes the overall form of films like *Scorpio* or *Invocation*. *Invocation*'s structure is jumbled and dissonant, an attack on the sensorium;[34] the entire piece is edited for abrasiveness, any residual flow is destroyed by spasms of electronic shock waves from Jagger's sound track. *Scorpio's* structure works from the inside out: from image to montage to montage-of-attractions to the whole as one entire montage system. The whole is purely a system of interrelationships and no attempt is made to impose an external order on this network. Image layers mount in density, implications, and velocity toward the climactic "rebel rouser" sequence when Scorpio, performing a black sabbath, transforms himself into his own demon brother and casts his death hex on the cycle rally which, through the montage, seems a swirling continuation of his ceremony of destruction. The use of montage-as-force-field reappears in *Lucifer's* invocation sequence—the aggressive vitality of tracking camera racing with the sorcerer's movements as he "widdershins" (runs counterclockwise) around a magic circle. These shots are intercut with an exterior long-shot of baby gorilla and tiger cub chasing around the base of a tree, the movements of nature coinciding with the "unnatural" counter-sun-wise dance of the magus filmmaker. But in this case the sequence is embedded in a less frenetic organization which makes up most of the film.

In *Lucifer* the camera at last liberates its subject matter from its usual medium-close-up iconography through a long-shot/long-take *mise-en-scène*. A series of landscapes, seascapes, skyscapes gain mythical proportions through long-take montage; the long shots establish the vastness of this universe. Lingering takes of the broken pharoah faces of the Colossus of Memnon have a quality of temporal displacement; they exist outside time and distance as defined by motion of either camera or subject. The impassive statues assume an ancient decadence, exhausted idols compared to the flesh of the living gods. This static vastness which the long-take/long-shot montage creates operates around a vortex or "core" of the film: the invocation sequence which gradually and erratically builds to a spinning force field of compressed energy. This disturbs and changes the natural universe of the film's structure: the exteriors are broken into by collage-inserts, then the external world reasserts itself with long, vertically dynamic takes and vertical wipes: nature rights herself and Lucifer is born.

The piece, as it stands, can be seen either as a complete work in itself or as a chapter with an appropriate ending to a forties science-fiction serial. The 1981 version has a film score composed by Bobby Beausoleil, recorded at Tracy Prison. The fragment presents a whole vision in itself. With *Lucifer* Anger breaks through his previous nihilism to a "happy ending" (the Crowleyan assertion of love and joy transcending sorrow and sin), dealing with larger, exterior concerns rather than dramas of occult exoticism and decadent ideology. The sun breaks through the clouds.

Conclusion

Films such as *Blonde Cobra* and *Flaming Creatures* placed an emphasis on themes which were common to those that had preoccupied Baudelaire and his successors, the Decadent/Symbolist artists of the late nineteenth century in France. Perverse and shocking, these films expressed an anti-naturalism and anti-materialism which the French artists had evolved a century earlier. Throughout all movements discussed in this study there runs the theme of "profound dissatisfaction with the deadening comforts of materialism."[1]

The films of the Baudelairean Cinema were revolutionary avant-garde works because of their celebrative condemnation of bourgeois society. Like the works of the surrealists, their form and content were profoundly shocking. In chapter 2 we examined the "shock technique" of Baudelaire in which the reader came into violent contact with the imagery. The same type of effect reverberates throughout the work of the Baudelairean filmmakers; apropos of this, Susan Sontag has written:

> . . . *Flaming Creatures* is a small but valuable work in a particular tradition, the poetic cinema of shock. In this tradition are to be found Buñuel's *Le Chien Andalou* and *L'age d'Or* . . . and the films of Kenneth Anger (*Fireworks, Scorpio Rising*) . . . [2]

However, although they rebelled against the technical and social conventions of the cinema, the Baudelairean filmmakers remained politically uncommitted. Unlike the surrealists, the Baudelairean filmmakers used socially subversive or morally offensive content without affiliating their work with political ideology.

Our study examined the work of three directors (henceforth referred to as "the Baudelaireans") within this cinematic trend: Jack Smith, Andy Warhol, and Kenneth Anger. While their thematic content is generally similar, their styles are markedly different. Anger is always in technical control of his material. Smith is far more slovenly, and Warhol abjured technique altogether. Unlike Smith and Warhol, Anger produced images that had a technical perfection and reflected high production values. Jack

Smith, on the other hand, used outdated stock, not even knowing what the result would be; Warhol constantly claimed that he could care less what the film looked like.

Their use of editing differs as well. Anger relied on complex montage systems; Smith merely cut from one sequence to the next; aside from sound/shock cuts, Warhol used no editing to speak of.

Each Baudelairean introduced unique cinematic styles. Warhol's *mise-en-scène* during his Baudelairean (or second) phase of filmmaking, used his earlier, minimalist camera technique applied to shocking verbal and visual content. Arthur Knight has pointed out that:

> It did not take Warhol long, however, to realize that this same technique, if applied to material with sexual connotations, could become not only more controversial but more commercial as well. Shortly, instead of a man eating a mushroom, he was showing a female impersonator eating—with obvious oral gratification—a banana. Instead of a middle-aged man getting a haircut, he showed a leather-jacketed youth getting—or at least responding to—a blow job . . . [3]

His static camera invited contemplation of blatantly shocking content; in the McLuhan sense, he used "cool" style to portray "hot" subject matter.

Of the three Baudelaireans, Jack Smith's vision is the most "frantic". He relies on the often erratic movements of both camera and characters to reveal sex as a form of heroic energy. Both his style and technique are shocking, and in this he is the Baudelairean with the strongest affinities to the surrealists. It could be said that he chaotically filmed chaos; we refer to Ken Kelman's description of such a vision: "*Flaming Creatures* might be subtitled Pandemonium Regained, a paean not for the Paradise Lost, but for the Hell Satan gained. Anger's Lucifer may be rising, but Smith's creatures writhe in ecstasy over the apocalpyse . . . "[4]

As established in chapter 5 of this text, Kenneth Anger is the most symbolist of the three Baudelaireans; his camera movements have been selected with great care in order to be integrated with the movement of the characters. Each element of his films is interwoven into a unique cinematic system of images and signs. Certainly Anger's *mise-en-scène* resembles a sort of palimpsest of synaesthetic correspondences. Like the symbolists, the Baudelaireans were primarily concerned with color, rhythm and other sensual phenomena in order to evoke a world of dreams and fantasy. More important than the synaesthetic correspondences were the transcendental correspondences. Baudelaire stated in his essay on Hugo, "everything is hieroglyphic," and later, "what is a poet (I am using the word in its broadest sense), if not a translator, a decipherer?"[5] In his later essay, "The Governance of the Imagination," Baudelaire then stated:

... the whole visible universe is nothing but a storehouse of images and signs, to which man's imagination will assign a place and relative value; it is a kind of pasture for the imagination to digest and transform.[6]

Anger's films operate on systems of correspondences, drawing together sensual forms and mystical/mythical content. This technique, which is also used in the films of Jack Smith and Ron Rice, totally replaced the narrative with abstract, visual sensuality.

The creatures, monsters and demons of Smith and Anger seem to have been influenced by Baudelaire's vampires and lesbians, Moreau's depictions of Salomé or the Sphinx, and Lautréamont's apocalyptic bestiary described in his novel *Maldoror*. In *Blonde Cobra* a title card is held up by the director. On it is scrawled a quote, "The city swarms with innocent monsters. Charles Baudelaire." (The phrase is recited on the soundtrack simultaneously.) These "monsters" cavort through the works of all the Baudelaireans. Just as Smith's characters were "creatures" and "monsters," Warhol's were "superstars". Almost all the Baudelairean characters express the horror of urban civilization and they reflect grotesque aberrations in bourgeois society. Warhol's actors/characters belonged to social subgroups (homosexuals, transvestites, transexuals, drug addicts, thieves, etc.), and, as Mekas originally pointed out, not unlike the characters to be found in de Sade, William Burroughs or Jean Genet.

Characters in Baudelairean films are often violently anti-social; Warhol's actors were exceptionally exhibitionistic, and certainly their characterizations were the most nihilistic and decadent. Baudelaire's character of the dandy was an expression of distaste for materialism and the industrial corruption of the nineteenth century. Later, the Decadent dandy became the personification of social decay. Of all the characters in the Baudelairean Cinema, the "superstars" best express this later type of corruption. They represent the concept of the Decadent dandy, jaded, hysterical and passive, preoccupied with sensory indulgence, stimulants and vivid fantasies. Incapable of retaining control over their environment, the dandies are preoccupied with giving themselves over to it entirely. Warhol, on the other hand, best embodies Baudelaire's concept of the dandy; one who remains aloof from a decadent environment in order to protect and cultivate his aesthetic. Warhol absents himself and yet examines his subjects intensely without touching or being touched by their psycho-dramas. His style is often static, his content is revolutionary, and, of all the Baudelaireans, his work incorporates the most Decadent/Symbolist themes. By this definition, he is the strongest and most influential Baudelairean in the movement.

This study has provided an extensive view of a trend in American avant-garde cinema. In order to substantially define and give a place to this trend it was necessary to draw from many different, and sometimes diverse, movements and schools. In the pursuit of an appropriate definition, we have ranged over two centuries, from Romanticism and Decadence/Symbolism, through surrealism and Pop Art. The films, literature, painting and theatre discussed here were carefully selected to illustrate the Baudelairean Cinema aesthetic; by gleaning and examining certain theories, themes, and techniques from the four art movements mentioned, we have arrived at a rich (albeit eclectic) definition of a cinematic trend.

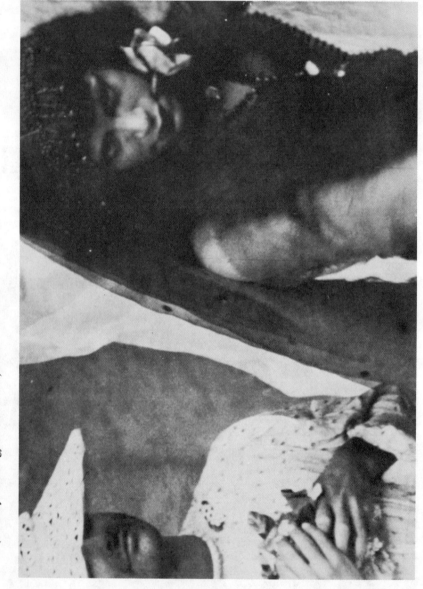

Fig. 2 Still from Jack Smith's *Flaming Creatures*
Smith in cameo role, 1., and Mario Montez in debut, r.
(Courtesy Anthology Film Archives)

Fig. 3. Frame enlargement, *Flaming Creatures* (Jack Smith)
(Courtesy Anthology Film Archives)

Fig. 4. Jack Smith's *Flaming Creatures*
(Courtesy Anthology Film Archives)

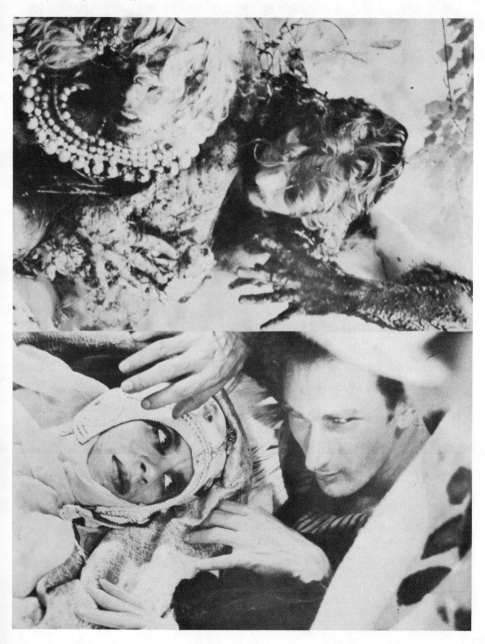

Fig. 6. (l. to r.): Taylor Mead, Jerry Joffen and Ron Rice, Summer 1962
       (Courtesy Anthology Film Archives)

Fig. 7. Ron Rice and Jack Smith
(Courtesy Anthology Film Archives)

Fig. 8. Ron Rice, Central Park, March 22, 1963
(Courtesy Anthology Film Archives)

Fig. 9. Ron Rice (production still from *Chumlum*)
(Courtesy Anthology Film Archives)

Fig. 10. Kenneth Anger (production still from *Scorpio Rising*)
(Courtesy Anthology Film Archives)

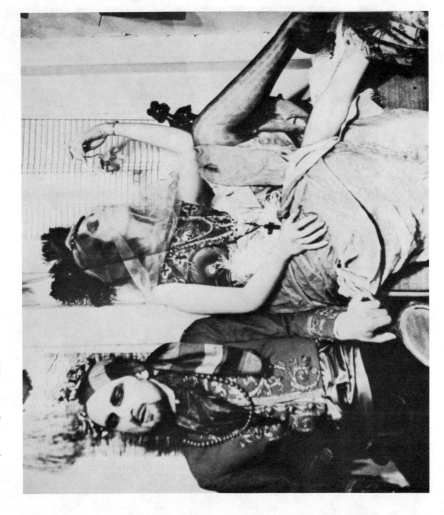

Fig. 11. Jack Smith and Linda Sampson in Bill Vehr's film "Brothel"
Photo by M. Zane-Safron
(Courtesy Anthology Film Archives)

Fig. 12. Frame enlargement, Kenneth Anger's *Fireworks* (Courtesy Anthology Film Archives)

Fig. 13. Andy Warhol at the Invisible Theatre, 1972
(Courtesy Anthology Film Archives)

Fig. 14. Still from Kenneth Anger's *Inauguration of the Pleasure Dome*
(Courtesy Anthology Film Archives)

Fig. 15. Portrait of Kenneth Anger superimposed on Gustave Duré etching,
Topanga Canyon, 1954
Photo: E. Teske
(Courtesy Anthology Film Archives)

Fig. 16. Frames from Kenneth Anger's *Lucifer Rising*: Isis (Courtesy Kenneth Anger)

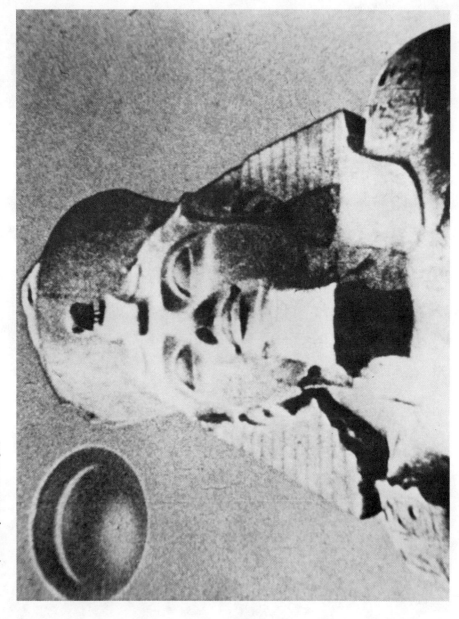

Fig. 17. End frame from Kenneth Anger's *Lucifer Rising*
(Courtesy Kenneth Anger)

Fig. 18. Andy Warhol
    Photo: Rupert Smith
    (Courtesy Andy Warhol Studio)

Fig. 19. Joe Spence and Ann Wehrer, *Bike Boy*, a story of a
motocyclist and his encounters with women
(Courtesy Andy Warhol Studio)

Fig. 20. Viva and Joe Spencer in a scene from *Bike Boy*, a film
in color by Andy Warhol
Photo: Factory Foto
(Courtesy Andy Warhol Studio)

Fig. 21. Viva and Joe Spencer in *Bike Boy*
Photo: Factory Foto
(Courtesy Andy Warhol Studio)

Fig. 22. Louis Waldon and Tom Hompertz in Andy Warhol's *Lonesome Cowboys* (Courtesy Andy Warhol Studio)

Fig. 23. Marie Menken and Gerard Malanga in Andy Warhol's *Chelsea Girls* (Courtesy Andy Warhol Studio)

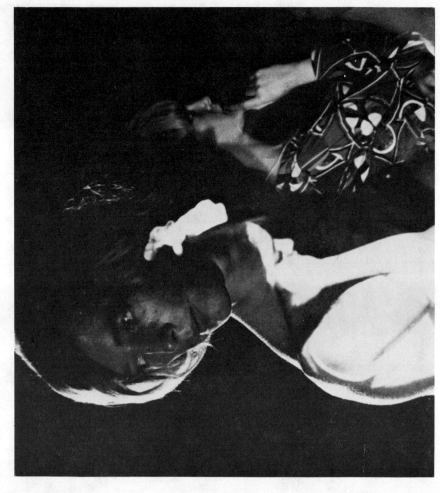

Fig. 24. Pepper Davis, International Velvet, and Ingrid Superstar in *Chelsea Girls* (Courtesy Andy Warhol Studio)

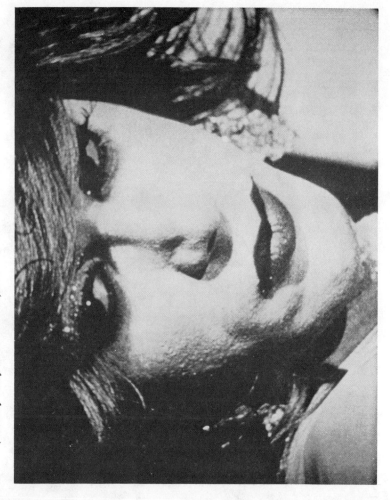

Fig. 25. Mario Montez in *Chelsea Girls*: Ed's Bed
Photo: Factory Foto
(Courtesy Andy Warhol Studio)

Fig. 26. Mario Montez in *Chelsea Girls*
(Courtesy Andy Warhol Studio)

Fig. 27. Mario Montez in *Chelsea Girls*
Photo: Factory Foto
(Courtesy Andy Warhol Studio)

Fig. 28. Gerard Malanga and Edie Sedgewick in Andy Warhol's *Vinyl*
(Courtesy Andy Warhol Studio)

Fig. 29. Nico, *Chelsea Girls*
     (Courtesy Andy Warhol Studio)

Fig. 30. Paul America in *My Hustler*
(Courtesy Andy Warhol Studio)

Fig. 31. John MacDermott and Paul America in *My Hustler* (Courtesy Andy Warhol Studio)

Fig. 32. Paul America in *My Hustler*
Photo: Factory Foto
(Courtesy Andy Warhol Studio)

Filmography

Looking back on 1963, one realizes that Jonas Mekas was only able to provide us with a limited list of examples of the Baudelairean Cinema. The following filmography makes a substantial addition to Mekas's list. Although there will be no effort made to justify every film in detail, each represents some of the characteristics common to the Baudelairean Cinema.

Several of the American avant-garde films and filmmakers of the 1960s included are not discussed in the main body of this text. Some of these films belong tangentially to the Baudelairean Cinema trend, but are important for their expression of the aesthetics defined throughout this study.

Many of these films have, at the time of this writing, become unavailable for viewing. It is of interest to note that, with the exception of the majority of films by Kenneth Anger, most of these films have been withdrawn from distribution by the filmmaker him/herself, for unknown reasons. For instance, all the extant Warhol films on this list had been withdrawn from U.S. distribution by 1975. Many other films have either been dropped from distribution or have changed booking agencies approximately once every two years; obviously it is of little use to include a list of possible distribution sources at this time.

The difficulty and, in many cases, impossibility of locating either a film or information regarding its present whereabouts did not influence our decision to include it. In some cases inclusion is based on screenings prior to a film's disappearance or access to substantial written descriptions. As is often the true case of experimental works of art, many of these films have been lost or destroyed. The various fates of these films are indicated by the following code:

*   lost
**   destroyed
***   unfinished
****   unavailable for unknown reasons

No asterisk indicates that the film is currently in 16mm distribution.

It might be said that the final irony of the Baudelairean Cinema is that it has destroyed itself.

Anger, Kenneth

1947–48   *Fireworks*: Camera by Chester Kessler. Sound. Music by Respighi: *Fountains of Rome*. 15 minutes. Black and white. With Kenneth Anger (The Dreamer), Bill Seltzer (Show Off), Gordon Gray (Body-bearing Sailor), members of the United States Navy.

    "A dissatisfied dreamer awakes, goes out into the night seeking 'a light', and is drawn through the needle's eye. A dream of a dream, he returns to a bed less empty than before."[1]

1949-70   *Puce Moment*: Camera by Kenneth Anger. Sound. Music by Jonathan Halper. 8 minutes. Color. With Yvonne Marquis as The Star. Filmed in Hollywood, California.
"Fragment of an unfinished film depicting the fantasy-lives of a suite of female film stars in Hollywood of the Twenties. The model here was Barbara LaMarr; her gowns and her villa (since demolished) provide the background."[2]

*The Love That Whirls***

1950-71   *Rabbit's Moon*: Camera by Kenneth Anger. Sound. Music by The Temptations and The Capris. 20 minutes. Black and white printed on color stock through a blue filter. With Jean Soubeyran as Pierrot.
"In a moonlit tinsel wood, Pierrot discovers a Magic Lantern. His new toy provokes disastrous consequences."[3]

1953   *Le Jeune Homme et la Mort*: Choreography by Roland Petit.
"A short version of Cocteau's ballet, now unshowable for copyright reasons."[4]

1953   *Eaux d'Artifice*: Camera by Kenneth Anger. Sound. Music by Vivaldi: *The Seasons*. 13 minutes. Ferrania Infra-Red printed on Ektachrome through a cyan filter. With Carmillo Salvatorelli as The Water Witch. Filmed in the gardens of the Villa D'Este, Tivoli, by the special permission of the Italian Department of Antiquities.
"Hide and seek in a night-time labyrinth of levels, cascades, balustrades, grottoes and ever-gushing fountains, until the Water Witch and the Fountain become one."[5]

1955   *Thelema Abbey*: Black and white.
"A short documentary on the restoration of murals at Aleister Crowley's Magick Headquarters."[6]****

1954-66   *Inauguration of the Pleasure Dome* (Sacred Mushroom Edition): Camera by Kenneth Anger. Sound. Music by Janacek. Printed by Kenneth Anger in hand lithography system on A, B, C, D and E rolls, on Ektachrome 7387. With Samson DeBrier (Lord Shiva, Osiris, Cagliostro, Nero, The Great Beast 666) Cameron (The Scarlet Woman, Lady Kali), Kathryn Kadell (Isis), Renata Loome (Lilith), Anais Nin (Astarte), Kenneth Anger (Hecate), the late Peter Loome (Ganymede).
"Lord Shiva, the Magician, wakes. A convocation of Theurgists in the guise of figures from mythology bearing gifts: The Scarlet Woman, Whore of Heavan, smokes a big fat joint; Astarte of the Moon brings the wings of snow; Pan bestows the bunch of Bacchus; Hecate offers the Sacred Mushroom, Yage, Wormwood brew. The vintage of Hecate is poured; Pan's cup is poisoned by Lord Shiva. The ORGIA ensues; a Magick masquerade party at which Pan is the prize. Lady Kali blesses the rites of the Children of Light as Lord Shiva invokes the Godhead with the formula, 'FORCE AND FIRE'. Dedicated to the Few; and to Aleister Crowley; and to the Crowned and Conquering Child."[7]

1959-61   *L'Histoire d'O*: Black and white.***

1964   *Scorpio Rising*: Camera by Kenneth Anger. Sound. Music by Ricky Nelson, Little Peggy March, The Angels, Bobby Vinton, The Crystals, The Ran-Dells, Kris Jensen, Claudine Clark, Gene McDaniels and The Surfaris. 31 minutes. color, printed on Ektachrome ER. With Bruce Byron (Scorpio), John Palone (Pin-Stripe), Ernie Allo (The Life of the Party), Johnny Sapienza (Taurus), Frank Carifi (Leo), Barry Rubin (Pledge), Steve Crandell (The Sissy Cyclist), Bill Dorfman (Brick Shit House), Jim Powers (Fallen Cyclist). Filmed in Brooklyn, Manhattan, and Walden's Pond, New York.

"A conjuration of the Presiding Princes, Angels and Spirits of the Spheres of MARS, formed as a 'high' view of the Myth of the American Motorcyclist. The Power Machine seen as a tribal totem, from toy to terror. Thanatos in chrome and black leather and bursting jeans. PART 1: Boys & Bolts; (masculine fascination with the Thing that Goes). PART 2: Image Maker (getting high on heroes: Dean's Rebel and Brando's Johnny; the true view of J.C.). PART 3: *Walpurgis* Party (J.C. Wallflower at the Cycler's Sabbath). PART 4: Rebel Rouser (the gathering of the Dark Legions, with a message from Our Sponsor). Dedicated to Jack Parson, Victor Childe, Jim Powers, James Dean, T.E. Lawrence, Hart Crane, Kurt Mann, The Society of Spartans, The Hell's Angels, and all overgrown boys who will ever follow the whistle of Love's Brother."[8]

1965–66   *Kustom Kar Kommandos*: Camera by Kenneth Anger. Sound. Music by the Parris Sisters. 3 minutes. Color, printed on Ektachrome. With The All-Chrome Ruby Plush Dream Buggy, and the maker. Filmed in San Bernadino, California.

"Excerpt from a work in progress. This sequence invokes the 'Dream Lover,' a blind for the Charioteer of the Tarot Trumps. Dedicated to Craig Breedlove."[9]

1969   *Invocation to My Demon Brother* (*Arrangement in Black and Gold*): Camera by Kenneth Anger and Judd Yalcut. Music composed by Mick Jagger on the Moog Synthesizer. Sound. 10 minutes. Color. With Speed Hacker (Wandbearer), Kenneth Anger (The Magus), Van Leuven (Acolyte), Harvey Bialy and Timotha (Brother and Sister of the Rainbow), Anton Szandor La Vey (His Satanic Majesty), Bobby Beausoleil (Lucifer). Filmed in San Francisco, California.

"Two boys lie sprawled naked on the blue bed. The Magus pauses in his whirl to soak them in fresh blood, then opens another wound. His eye falls on the blood-soaked chest of the blond. It is branded with a swastika. He grabs it and begins to whirl it around the world.

'That hurt,' the black boy screams.

'You need to hurt,' the Magus laughed.

'It gives you Anger.'

The shadowing forth of Our Lord Lucifer, as the Powers of Darkness gather at a midnight mass. The dance of the Magus widdershins around the Swirling Spiral Force, the solar swastika, until the Bringer of Light—Lucifer—breaks through."[10]

1974   *Lucifer Rising* (Part One of a Work in Progress): Camera by Kenneth Anger, Noel Burch, Michael Cooper and others. Sound. Music composed by Jimmy Page. 30 minutes. Color. The invocation (Part Two), and dynasty (Part Three) of Lucifer's reign on Earth. [See text for full description.] With Myriam Gabril (Isis), Donald Cammel (Osiris), Marianne Faithfull (Lilith), Kenneth Anger (The Magus), Leslie Huggins (Lucifer). Filmed in England, Egypt, Germany, Switzerland, France, and America.

Jacobs, Ken

1957   *Little Cobra Dance*: Camera by Ken Jacobs.

". . . Showed Smith dressed as a Spanish lady doing a frenetic dance, falling down, and being questioned by the police,the last being an actual event incorporated into the film."[11]

1957?   *Star Spangled to Death*: Camera by Ken Jacobs. Silent. 3 hours. Color and black and white. With Jack Smith and Jerry Simms.

"I would just move toward some ordered situation and then introduce Jack or Jerry to break up its pattern or to create some new possibilities of patterns that my mind would not have come up with. I felt the chaos of those two individuals and my penchant for a pattern clarified each other; the patterns became clearer because of the chaos, in the midst of the chaos; these two bodies of chaos became clearer because of the pattern.

". . . I was interested in revealing things in their breaking and I wanted *Star Spangled to Death* to be a film that was constantly breaking.

". . . the film was so torturously long that most of the audience walked out when versions were shown."[12]****

1958-63   *Little Stabs at Happiness*: Camera by Ken Jacobs. Sound. 10 minutes. Color. Jack Smith and long-lost friends cavort in New York City. Smith dances on rooftops dressed as a baby.

"The first episode shows Smith and a girl sitting in a dry bathtub playing with dolls. At one point he tries to eat the crotch of a doll between puffs of a cigarette. The camera moves casually, often resting on a bare lightbulb or another static element in the room."[13]

1959-62   *Blonde Cobra*: Camera by Bob Fleischner and Jack Smith. Edited by Ken Jacobs. Sound. Music by Jerome Kern; live radio music. Black and white. Smith and Simms perform a series of pantomimes in a cramped set of a N.Y.C. loft. Smith narrates several stories, dreams and fragments over visuals and black leader; simulates suicide, and, dressed in baby clothes, smashes radios (to the accompaniment of live radio in the audience).

". . . another sordid episode in this mock quest for sexual identity."[14]

The first "Baudelairean" films (so called by Jonas Mekas). With Jack Smith and Jerry Simms.

1961   *The Death of P'Town*: Camera by Ken Jacobs and Jack Smith. 5 minutes. Black and white.

". . . showed frolics among dunes and cemeteries, with Jack Smith dressed as The Fairy Vampire. This was the last film Jacobs did with Smith. A subsequent work, *Baudelairean Capers* (1963), was marred by defective equipment and film stock, and is unfinished. And at this point, his 16mm camera was stolen, resulting in a switch to 8mm."[15]

Lederberg, Dov

196?   *Eargogh*: Camera by Dov Lederberg. 30 minutes. Color. Marie Menken plays a prostitute for whom Jack Smith, as Vincent Van Gogh, cuts off his ear.[16]***

Rice, Ron

1964   *The Queen of Sheba Meets the Atom Man*: Camera by Ron Rice. Silent. Black and white. With Taylor Mead, Jack Smith, Winifred Bryan.

"He [Rice] did not live to complete the editing . . . Bryan (a colossal black woman) plays an alcoholic odalisque . . . Taylor Mead's encounter with many household objects . . . a spoof on *Hamlet* with Jack Smith as The Prince, and a direct take-off on Gregory Markopoulos' *Twice A Man*."[17]

1964   *Chumlum*: Camera by Ron Rice and Jack Smith. Sound. Music by Angus MacLise. 26 minutes. Color. With Jack Smith, Frankie Francine, Mario Montez, and Joel Markman.
". . . An Arabian Nights vision of a palace brothel, inspired by Jerry Joffen and Jack Smith. In it, gorgeously costumed characters surrounded by diaphanous draperies, fumble through vague and erotic acts in hammocks. Much use is made of superimpositions, creating a sensual flow of color and space."[18]

Smith, Jack

1962   *Scotchtape*: Camera by Jack Smith. Sound. Music: 78 r.p.m. Latin pop music (composers unknown). 3 minutes. Color. With Jack Smith and Jerry Simms.
". . . made . . . during the shooting of *Star Spangled to Death*. That day Jacobs had assembled his cast in a destroyed building or a section of a junkyard. Rusted cables in great tangles and broken slabs of concrete were all about . . . . "[19]

1962–63   *Flaming Creatures*: Camera by Jack Smith and Jerry Joffen. Sound. Music: Latin pop music (composers unknown) taken from 78 r.p.m. records. 60 minutes. Black and white; shot on outdated Dupont negative stock. With Francine Francine, Jack Smith, Joel Markman (The Vampire Monroe), Jerry Simms (Sailor), Naomi Levine (Dark Lady), Mario Montez (Spanish Dancer).
". . . in *Flaming Creatures*, a couple of women and a much larger number of men, most of them clad in flamboyant thrift-shop women's clothes, frolic about, pose and posture, dance with one another, enact various scenes of voluptuousness, sexual frenzy, romance, and vampirism . . . the group rape of a bosomy young woman, rape happily converting itself into an orgy. Of course *Flaming Creatures* is outrageous, and intends to be. The very title tells us that."[20]

1963–64   *The Great Pasty Triumph* or *Normal Love*: Camera by Jack Smith. Silent. Color, shot on outdated Agfa-Gavaertchrome. With Francine Francine (The Yellow Hag), Mario Montez (Marilyn-the-Mermaid), Beverly Grant (The Cobra Woman), Tiny Tim (The Werewolf), Angus MacLise (The Mummy), Diane De Prima (The Pregnant Woman), John Vaccaro (The White Bat), Naomi Levine, Jack Smith, and Andy Warhol.
"In the rough cut that he [Smith] exhibited in 1964, it was a paratactic parade of episodes describing a pantheon of monsters from horror films . . . . The projection of the rushes of these scenes throughout 1963 at midnight after the programs of the Film-Makers' Cinematheque or in Ron Rice's loft was the occasion for important meetings of film-makers, actors, and critics. Each episode was a self-contained, sensuous exploration of a simple event structured by scene, photographed of outdated color stock that produced ravishing expanses of pastel greens, pinks and blues . . . . see the green mummy wading after a nude girl in a pond of waterlilies; the Mermaid taking a milk bath or having a mud-throwing fight with the Werewolf; a pier covered with the bodies of dead or sleeping transvestites in pink gowns projecting into the azure sea; the emerald Cobra Woman exploring a dark cave; a watermelon feast; a giant pink birthday cake with half a dozen creatures dancing on it, including a very pregnant woman."[21]****

1964-65   *No President*: Camera by Jack Smith. 100 minutes. Intercutting between erotic tableaux of creatures and a documentary on Wendell Wilkie's life.***

Sonbert, Warren

1964   *Amphetamine*: Camera by Warren Sonbert. Sound. Music by The Supremes. 10 minutes. Black and white. An insidious little film which critic James Stoller has called "a heart stopper."[22] Loop-like repetitions of adolescent junkies concentrating on their fixes, each caught in similar framing, cut together in jump-cut fashion, all more or less locked into the continuous "rush" while, on the soundtrack, The Supremes keep asking, "Where Did Our Love Go?"; a powerfully cyclic montage of these adolescent boys fixing, nodding and embracing; the film imparts a feeling of existence replaced.

1966   *Where Did Our Love Go?*: Camera by Warren Sonbert. Sound: ¼ inch tape, 7½ i.p.s. 15 minutes. Color.
        "It is . . . a randomly edited 'home movie' in which the people I care for the most are inextricably linked together, flowing from one to another . . . . The film is about the glamour of New York . . . . New York is the nostalgia of the present . . . . For the soundtrack I used mostly old rock and roll—the most nostalgic music there is."[23]

1966   *Hall of Mirrors*: Camera by Warren Sonbert. Soundtrack: "Don't Walk Away, Rene" (Left Bank). Theme music from Godard's *Le Mepris* (George Delerue). 10 minutes. Color. With Rene Ricard and Gerard Malanga.
        Triptych of Hollywood out-takes. Rene Ricard, alone and crying, and Georges Malanga pacing the Lucas Samaras's mirror room at the Albright Knox museum.
        A haunting little film; Sonbert's most Baudelairean work.

1966-67   *The Bad the the Beautiful*: Camera by Warren Sonbert. No further technical information available.
        "Favored Manhattan scenes and the beautiful and vacant children who inhabit them."[24] This film originated as ten rolls of film of ten couples spending the day in collaboration with the filmmaker.****

Comment:
There is a unique ease with which Sonbert captures his Manhattan society friends at play in boutiques, museums and penthouses. HIs shooting style is one in which the camera doesn't linger over, but casually caresses its subjects as though reluctant to become too involved with the exceptionally photogenic. This is cinema with the power of a glance, slightly disengaged. It is this "dandy-esque" quality and Sonbert's involvement with expressing nostalgia which defines these works of his as Baudelairean.

Vehr, Bill

196?   *Lil Picard's Beauty Environment of the Year 2105*: No Available Information. With Mario Montez.****

196?   *The Mystery of the Spanish Lady*: No available information. With Jack Smith and Mario Montez.****

1965   *Brothel: Tangiers Dream Cycle*: No available information. With Jack Smith and
         Mario Montez.****

1966   *Avocada*: No available information. With Jack Smith and Mario Montez.****

         Comments:
         "The suggestions and the combinations of sexual provocation and feeling of
         mystery can create eroticism, as in Bill Vehr's *Avocada*, or his *Brothel*, which
         stresses erotic fantasy by the use of rich contrast of flesh, extravagant textures and
         colors to make a tapestry of erotic sensations."[25]
         ". . . *Avocada* and *Brothel* emphasize affinities with Hollywood. His writhing
         woman in *Avocada* mimics the exaggerated, perverse (because of the implicit
         unnatural restraints of censorship) body movements of a 'movie star' in torment
         . . . . Vehr, like Smith, works equally in the theatre, being a member of the
         Vaccaro, Tavel and Ludlam Theatre of the Ridiculous . . . . "[26]

Warhol, Andy

         For information on these films selected from the work of Andy Warhol, we draw
         directly from Stephen Koch's filmography from his book, *Stargazer: Andy
         Warhol's World and His Films*.[27] Descriptions of films are given only where
         sufficient sources were available.

1963   *Andy Warhol Films Jack Smith Filming "Normal Love"*: Camera by Andy
         Warhol. Silent. 3 minutes. Color.
         "A 'newsreel' film showing Jack Smith shooting *Normal Love*. The original was
         seized by the New York Police in March 1964, together with Jean Genet's film, *Un
         Chant d'Amour*. The fate of the original is unknown. No print exists."****

1964   *Batman Dracula*: Camera by Andy Warhol. Silent. 2 hours. Black and white.
         Filmed on the beaches of Long Island and on the roof of the factory. With Jack
         Smith (Dracula), Baby Jane Holzer, Beverly Grant, Ivy Nicholson.
         "Stills indicate that it was very much influenced by the style of Jack Smith."***

1964   *Harlot*: Warhol's first sound-sync film. 70 minutes. Black and white. With Gerard
         Malanga, Philip Fagan, Carol Koshinskie, Mario Montez. Out-of-frame dialogue
         by Ronald Tavel, Harry Fainlight, Billy Linich.
         A transvestite plays Jean Harlow in ". . . a near orgy of banana consump-
         tion."****

1965   *Suicide*: Co-directed by Chuck Wein. Sound. 70 minutes. Color. Scenario and
         extemporaneous dialogue by Ronald Tavel. With Mario Montez.****
         A man's account of an attempted suicide as the camera stares for a very long
         time at his scarred wrists.****

1965   *Screen Test #1*: Sound. 70 minutes. Black and white. Scenario by Ronald Tavel.
         With Philip Fagin.****

1965   *Screen Test #2*: Sound. 70 minutes. Black and white. Scenario by Ronald Tavel.
         Out-of-frame dialogue by Ronald Tavel. With Mario Montez.****

1965   *The Life of Juanita Castro*: Sound. 70 minutes. Black and white. Scenario by Ronald Tavel. With Marie Mencken (Juanita), Elecktrah (Raoul), Waldo Diaz Balart, Mercedes Ospina, Manina Ospina, Ronald Tavel.****

1965   *Drunk*: Sound. 70 minutes. Black and white. Scenario by Ronald Tavel. With Larry Latrae, Gregory Battcock, Daniel Cassidy, T. Carillo.****

1965   *Horse*: Sound. 106 minutes. Black and white. Scenario by Ronald Tavel. With Larry Latrae, Gregory Battcock, Daniel Cassidy, Jr.****

1965   *Poor Little Rich Girl*: Co-directed by Chuck Wein. Sound. 70 minutes. Black and white. Edie Sedgewick tells of her inheritance: she has lost it.****

1965   *Vinyl*: Camera by Bud Wirtschafter. Sound. 70 minutes. Scenario by Ronald Tavel. Filmed version of Tavel's adaptation of Anthony Burgess's *A Clockwork Orange*. Brechtian tableaux of sexual violence. Gerard Malanga dances with whips and chains, is arrested, and tortured by scientists. With Gerard Malanga, Edie Sedgewick, Ondine, Tosh Carillo, Larry Latrae, Jacques Potin, John MacDermott, and others.

1965   *Bitch*: Sound. 70 minutes. Black and white. Filmed immediately after *Vinyl*. Exists in original only. With Gerard Malanga, Marie Mencken, Willard Maas, Edie Sedgewick.****

1965   *Restaurant*: Co-directed and co-scripted by Chuck Wein. Sound. 35 minutes. Black and white. With Edie Sedgewick and Ondine.
        This film should not be confused with *Nude Restaurant*, or a second film called *Restaurant* both of which were shot at the same time in October 1967.****

1965   *Kitchen*: Sound. 70 minutes. Black and white. With Edie Sedgewick, Roger Trudeau, Donald Lyons, Elecktrah, David MacCabe, Rene Richard.
        Film which introduced the concept of "superstar". Dialogue scenes of personal confrontation—later developed fully in *Chelsea Girls*.****

1965   *Beauty #2*: Co-directed and co-scripted by Chuck Wein. Sound. 70 minutes. Black and white. With Edie Sedgewick, Gino Peschio, and, out-of-frame, Gerard Malanga and Chuck Wein.
        A study of Edie Sedgewick barely reacting to the taunts of male cast members. Simulated sex; long monologue on her horror of death.

1965   *My Hustler*: Co-directed by Chuck Wein. Sound. 70 minutes. Black and white. With Paul America, Ed Hood, John MacDermott, Genevieve Charbon, Joseph Campbell, Dorothy Dean.
        First "psychological realism" drama. Three neighbors on Fire Island take turns trying to seduce a male prostitute.****

1965   *Camp*: Sound. 70 minutes. Black and white. With Paul Swan, Baby Jane Holzer, Mar-Mar Donyle, Jodie Babs, Tally Brown, Jack Smith, Fu-Fu Smith, Tosh Carillo, Mario Montez, Gerard Malanga.
        An Underground review; describing Jack Smith's performance, Stephen Koch wrote: ". . . surely among the strangest and most bizarre anywhere in film . . . . Perversely executed by Smith . . . to force Warhol to move the camera."

1965   *Hedy* (also known as *The Most Beautiful Girl in the World*, *The Shoplifter*, or *The Fourteen Year Old Girl*): Sound. 70 minutes. Music by John Cale and Louis Reed. Black and white. With Mario Montez, Mary Woronow, Harvey Tavel, Ingrid Superstar, Ronald Tavel, Gerard Malanga, Rick Lockwood, James Claire, Randy Borscheidt, David Meyers, Jack Smith, Arnold Rockwood.

      Based on a series of real and fictional incidents in the life of Hedy La Marr—she has a face-lift, shoplifts in a department store, is caught and interrogated by the store detective. The film ends with a tour of the star's home.****

1965   *More Milk Yvette* (also known as *Lana Turner*): Scenario by Ronald Tavel. Sound. 70 minutes. Black and white. With Mario Montez, Paul Caruso, Richard Schmidt.****

1966   *The Velvet Underground and Nico*: Sound. 70 minutes. Black and white.

      "Andy Warhol's rock and roll electronic group presenting a 70 minute symphony of sound broken up by the New York Police."—Gerard Malanga.****

1966   *The Chelsea Girls*: Camera by Andy Warhol and others. Sound. 3½ hours on twin-screens—total film time: 7 hours. 12 reels. Color and black and white.

      Includes: *The Bed*, *The John*, *The Trip*, *The Duchess*, *Hanoi Hanna*, *The Pope Ondine Story*, *The Gerard Malanga Story*, *Their Town (Toby Short)*;

      The Gerard Malanga Story: With Marie Menken, Mary Woronow, Gerard Malanga.

      Hanoi Hanna (*Queen of China*): Written by Ronald Tavel. With Mary Woronow, "International Velvet", Ingrid Superstar, Angelina "Pepper" Davis.

      The Pope Ondine Story: With Bob "Ondine" Olivio, Angeline "Pepper" Davis, Ingrid Superstar, Alberte Rene Richard, Mary Woronow, "International Velvet", Ronna.

      The John: With Ed Hood, Patrick Fleming, Mario Montez, Angelina "Pepper" Davis, "International Velvet", Mary Woronow, Gerard Malanga, Rene Richard, Ingrid Superstar.

      Their Town: With Eric Emerson. Strobe lighting by Billy Linich.

      Each reel is unedited and of identical length; all have soundtracks; eight are in black and white, four are in color. In his style of psycho-realism Warhol engages a small repertory of Underground personalities in a series of confrontations and undirected emotional explosions. Much of the acting is stylized boredom or anxiety. Concerning the acting, Koch wrote: "Finally, this cinematic spectacle is about the self-containment of a certain elegant discretion, the discretion of Baudelaire's dandy."

      Steven Dwoskin calls this film: ". . . a major catalyst between the Underground and the Overground, grossing ten to fifteen thousand dollars a week during its run."

1967   *The Loves of Ondine*: Sound. 86 minutes. Color. With Ondine, Viva, Joe Dallesandro, Angelina Davis, Brigid Polk, Ivy Nicholson, and numerous unidentified men.

1967   *I, A Man*: Sound. 100 minutes. Black and white. With Tom Baker, Ivy Nicholson, Ingrid Superstar, Valerie Solanis, Cynthia May, Bettina Coffin, Ultra Violet, Nico.****

1967   *Bike Boy*: Sound. 96 minutes. Color. With Joe Spencer, Viva, Ed Weiner, Brigid Polk, Ingrid Superstar.****

1967   *Nude Restaurant*: Sound. No time known. Color. With Viva, Taylor Mead, Louis Waldron, Alan Midgette, Ingrid Superstar, Julian Burroughs, and others.

1967   *Lonesome Cowboys*: Camera by Andy Warhol. Sound. 110 minutes. Color.
            A parody, shot in the style of documentary realism, of a Hollywood Western, shot on location at Old Tucson, Arizona. A "Western about sex," very loosely based on Shakespeare's *Romeo and Juliet*. The last film shot by Warhol.****

Appendix A

On the Baudelairean Cinema

Jonas Mekas, "Movie Journal," *The Village Voice*, May 2, 1963.

There are many good reasons for barking about it. Lately, several movies have appeared from the underground which, I think, are marking a very important turn in independent cinema. As *Shadows* and *Pull My Daisy* marked the end of the avant-garde-experimental cinema tradition of the 40's and 50's (the symbolist/surrealist cinema of intellectual meanings), now there are works appearing which are marking a turn in the so-called New American Cinema—a turn from the New York realist school (the cinema of "surface" meanings and social engagement) towards a cinema of disengagement and new freedom.

The movies I have in mind are Ron Rice's *The Queen of Sheba Meets the Atom Man*; Jack Smith's *The Flaming Creatures*; Ken Jacobs' *Little Stabs at Happiness*; Bob Fleischner's *Blonde Cobra*—four works that make up the real revolution in cinema today. These movies are illuminating and opening up sensibilities and experiences never before recorded in the American arts; a content which Baudelaire, the Marquis de Sade, and Rimbaud gave to world literature a century ago and which Burroughs gave to American literature three years ago. It is a world of flowers of evil, of illumination, of torn and tortured flesh; a poetry which is at once beautiful and terrible, good and evil, delicate and dirty.

A thing that may scare an average viewer is that this cinema is treading on the very edge of perversity. These artists are without inhibitions, sexual or any other kind. These are, as Ken Jacobs put it, "dirty-mouthed" films. They all contain homosexual and lesbian elements. The homosexuality, because of its existence outside the official moral conventions, has unleashed sensitivities and experiences which have been at the bottom of much great poetry since the beginning of humanity.

Blonde Cobra, undoubtedly, is the masterpiece of the Baudelairean cinema, and it is a work hardly surpassable in perversity, in richness, in beauty, in sadness, in tragedy. I think it is one of the great works of personal cinema, so personal that it is ridiculous to talk about "author's" cinema. I know that the larger public will misinterpret and misunderstand these films. As there are poets appreciated only by other poets (William Carlos Williams was such a poet for many years), so there is now a cinema for the few, too terrible and too "decadent" for an "average" man in any organized culture. But then, if everybody would dig Baudelaire, or Sade, or Burroughs, my God where would humanity be?

Appendix B

Major Pop Songs in Kenneth Anger Films

1. "Dream Lover," The Parris Sisters (1964), Atco.

2. "I Will Follow Him," Little Peggy March (1963), RCA Victor.

3. "He's A Rebel," The Crystals (1962), Philles.

4. "Fools Rush In," Ricky Nelson (1964), Decca.

5. "Wipeout," The Surfaris (1963), Dot.

6. "Blue Velvet," Bobby Vinton (1963), Epic.

7. "I Only Have Eyes For You," The Temptations (1964), Gordy.

8. "I'm A Hermit," Jonathan Halper

9. "Leaving My Old Life Behind," Jonathan Halper.

10. "Party Lights," Claudine Clark (1962), Chancellor.

11. "Wind-Up Doll," The Ran-Dells (1963), Decca.

12. "You're The Devil In Disguise," Elvis Presley (1963), RCA Victor.

13. "My Boyfriend's Back," The Angels (1963), Smash.

14. "Heat Wave," Martha & The Vandellas (1963), Gordy.

15. "Hit The Road, Jack," Ray Charles (1961), ABC-Paramount.

Notes

Introduction

1. Susan Sontag, *Against Interpretation and Other Essays* (New York: Dell Publishing Co., Inc., 1966), pp. 229–34.

2. Andrew Sarris, *The Village Voice* (New York), 17 May 1976, p. 132.

3. Jonas Mekas, *Movie Journal: The Rise of a New American Cinema, 1959–1971* (New York: The Macmillan Press, 1972), pp. 111–16.

4. Ibid., p. 115.

5. Ibid., p. 112.

6. Gregory Battcock, ed., *The New American Cinema: A Critical Anthology* (New York: E. P. Dutton & Co., Inc.), p. 8. This quote first appeared in print in the Ken Kelman article "Smith Myth," in *Film Culture* 29, (Summer 1963), pp. 3–4.

7. Mekas, *Movie Journal*, pp. 111–16.

Chapter 1

1. Jonas Mekas, "The Irresponsibility of My Colleague Film Critics, On the Baudelairean Cinema," *The Village Voice*, 2 May 1963, cited in Jonas Mekas, *Movie Journal*, pp. 84–86.

2. Paul Adams Sitney, *Visionary Film: The American Avant-Garde* (New York: Oxford University Press, Inc., 1974), p. 379.

3. "There is one more term that is used interchangeably with "the underground." This is "the New American Cinema." It is derived from the New American Cinema Group, an organization founded in [September of] 1960 by a number of independent film-makers whose work ranged from the commercial to the avant-garde. The New American Cinema takes in the underground film, but is broader than it. It is the total rebellion in the United States against the domination of film by Hollywood and other commercial factors." Sheldon Renan, *An Introduction to the American Underground Film: A Unique, Fully Illustrated Handbook to the Art of Underground Films and Their Makers* (New York: E. P. Dutton & Co., Inc., 1967), p. 23.

4. Jonas Mekas, "A Call For a New Generation of Film Makers," *Film Culture* 19 (Summer 1959), p. 1.

5. Stephen Dwoskin, *Film Is: The International Free Cinema* (London: Peter Owen Limited, 1975), p. 59.

6. Sitney, *Visionary Film*, p. 385.

7. Farber identifies Underground films as "Neither experimental, liberal, slick, spectacular, low-budget, epical, improving, or flagrantly commercial like Sam Katzman two-bitters. They are faceless movies. . . . Tight, cliché-ridden melodramas about stock musclemen." Farber felt that the films were "Underground," because the director "hides out in sub-surface reaches of his work," and that the theatres in which these films were shown were "caves . . . murky, congested theatres, looking like glorified tattoo parlors on the outside. . . ." Manny Farber, "Underground Films," *Commentary* (1957), cited in Manny Farber, *On Movies* (New York: The Stonehill Publishing Company, 1971), pp. 15–16.

8. Stan VanDerBeek, "The Cinema Delimina: Films from the Underground," *Film Quarterly* 14 (Summer 1961), pp. 5–15.

9. Renan, *Introduction to Underground Film*, p. 17.

10. Ibid., p. 22

11. Dwoskin, *Film Is,* p. 24.

12. Renan, *Introduction to Underground Film*, p. 25.

13. Stephen Koch, *Stargazer: Andy Warhol's World and His Films* (New York: Praeger Publishers, Inc., 1973), p. 45.

14. Jonas Mekas, "On Cinéma Vérité, Ricky Leacock, and Warhol," *The Village Voice*, 13 August 1964, cited in Mekas, *Movie Journal*, p. 154.

15. Jonas Mekas, "On the Mystery of the Low-Budget 'Art' Film, Emergence of the Underground Star Cinema," *The Village Voice*, 20 February 1964, cited in Mekas, *Movie Journal*, p. 121.

16. *The Beat Generation*, cited from "For *Shadows*, Against *Pull My Daisy*: An Argument by Parker Tyler," *Film Culture* 24 (Spring 1962), pp. 28–34.

17. Dwoskin, *Film Is,* p. 50.

18. Renan, *Introduction to Underground Film*, p. 36.

19. The scenarios and extemporaneous dialogue for these Warhol films were written by Ronald Tavel:

Suicide	1965
Screen Test #1	1965
Screen Test #2	1965
The Life of Juanita Castro	1965
Drunk	1965
Horse	1965
Poor Little Rich Girl	1965
Vinyl	1965
Hedy (also known as *The Most Beautiful Woman in the World, The Shoplifter,* or *The Fourteen Year Old Girl*)	1965
Hanoi Hanna (Queen of China): Segment of *The Chelsea Girls*	1966

20. Mekas, *Movie Journal*, p. 121.

21. Sitney, *Visionary Film*, p. 383.

22. Jonas Mekas, "Notes on the New American Cinema," *Film Culture* 24 (Spring 1962), p. 12.

23. Sontag, *Against Interpretation*, p. 231

24. Ibid., p. 231.

25. Jonas Mekas, "On How the Underground Fooled Hollywood," *The Village Voice*, 21 December 1967, cited in Mekas, *Movie Journal*, p. 302.

26. Renan, *Introduction to Underground Film*, p. 49.

27. Mekas, "Notes on New Cinema," p. 13.

28. Jim Kitses, *Horizons West: Anthony Mann, Budd Boetticher, Sam Peckinpah: Studies of Authorship within the Western* (London: Indiana University Press in association with *Sight and Sound* (London) and the Education Department of the British Film Institute, 1969), p. 14.

29. Joris-Karl Huysmans, *A rebours*, Introduction by Havelock Ellis, trans. unknown (New York: Three Sirens Press, 1931), p. xlix.

30. Sontag, *Against Interpretation*, p. 231.

31. Ibid., p. 234.

32. Ibid., p. 279.

33. Ibid., p. 280.

34. Ibid.

35. Ibid., p. 281.

36. Ibid.

37. Ibid., p. 283.

38. Ibid., p. 282.

39. Charles Pierre Baudelaire, *Les Fleurs du Mal*, first published in June 1857 by Poulet-Malassis, Paris.

40. David Curtis, "English Avant-Garde Film: An Early Chronology," *Studio International Journal* (London) 190 (November-December 1975): 978.

41. Jonas Mekas, "The Year 1964," *The Village Voice*, 7 January 1965, cited in Mekas, *Movie Journal*, p. 173.

42. Jonas Mekas, "On the Misery of Community Standards," *The Village Voice*, 18 June 1964, cited in Mekas, *Movie Journal*, p. 141.

43. Jonas Mekas, "The Supreme Obscenity of the United States Congress," *The Village Voice*, 15 August 1968, cited in Mekas, *Movie Journal*, p. 316.

Chapter 2

1. John Middleton Murry, "Baudelaire," in *Baudelaire: A Collection of Critical Essays*, ed. Henri Peyre (Englewood Cliffs, N.J.: Prentice-Hall, Inc., 1962), p. 95.

2. Charles Baudelaire, "New Notes on Edgar Poe," in *Baudelaire as a Literary Critic*, ed. and trans. Lois H. Hyslop and Francis E. Hyslop, Jr. (University Park: The Pennsylvania University Press, 1964), p. 122.

3. Frank Kermode, *Romantic Image* (New York: Alfred A. Knopf. Inc., and Random House, Inc., 1957), p. 5.

4. In "Le Peintre de la vie moderne," his study of Dutch painter Constantin Guys, Baudelaire subtitled his third chapter "An Artist, Man of the World, Man of Crowds, and Child." He had also translated E. A. Poe's short story "The Man of the Crowd" (L'homme des foules) in *Le Pay* (January 28-30, 1855). Cited in Marcel Ruff, *Baudelaire*, trans. Agnes Kertesz (New York: New York University Press, 1966), p. 180.

5. Charles Baudelaire, "The Painter of Modern Life," in *Baudelaire: Selected Writings on Art and Artists*, ed. and trans. P. E. Charvet (Baltimore: Penguin Books, Inc., 1972), p. 400.

6. Charles Baudelaire, "Draft of Preface for *Les Fleurs du mal*," in *The Flowers of Evil*, ed. Marthiel and Jackson Mathews (New York: New Directions Publishing Corp., 1955), p. xxix.

7. Walter Benjamin, *Charles Baudelaire: A Lyric Poet in the Era of High Capitalism*, trans. Harry Zohn (London: NLB, 1973), p. 59.

8. Ibid., p. 117.

9. Charles Baudelaire, *Intimate Journals*, trans. Christopher Isherwood, with an introduction by W. H. Auden (Boston: Beacon Press, 1957), p. 17.

10. Théophile Gautier, Preface to *Mademoiselle de Maupin*, trans. and ed. Professor F. C. De Sumichrast (New York: C. T. Brainard Publishing Co., 1900), pp. 81-82.

11. Baudelaire, "Théophile Gautier," in *Baudelaire as a Literary Critic*, p. 161.

12. Baudelaire, *The Flowers of Evil*, ed. Mathews, p. xxvi.

13. Baudelaire, "The Queen of the Faculties," in *Baudelaire as a Literary Critic*, p. 180.

14. Mario Praz, *The Romantic Agony*, trans. Angus Davidson (London: Oxford University Press, 1951), p. 143.

15. Je m'avance à l'attaque, et je grimpe aux assauts,
    Comme après un cadavre un choeur de vermisseaux,
    Et je chéris, ô bête implacable et cruelle,
    Jusqu'à cette froideur par où tu m'es plus belle!
    "La Chevelure," cited in *Flowers of Evil*, ed. Mathews, p. 260. English translation in text translated by Graham Reynolds, cited in *Flowers of Evil*, ed. Mathews, p. 33.

16. Baudelaire, *Baudelaire as a Literary Critic*, p. xxvi.

17. Praz, *The Romantic Agony*, p. 57.

18. Ruff, *Baudelaire*, p. 94.

19. "Le Peintre de la vie moderne," was first published in 1863 even though Baudelaire had completed the essay three years earlier. First published in *Le Figaro* (November 26, 28 and December 3). Cited in Ruff, *Baudelaire*, p. 188.

20. Ruff, *Baudelaire*, p. 143.

21. Ibid., p. 143.

22. Baudelaire, *Selected Writings*, p. 420.

23. Ibid., p. 421.

24. Baudelaire, "Exposition Universelle 1855," *Baudelaire as a Literary Critic*, p. 82.

25. Baudelaire, "The Painter of Modern Life," *Selected Writings*, p. 421.

26. Baudelaire, *Intimate Journals*, pp. 11–12.

27. Praz, *Romantic Agony*, p. 56. Praz cites Tillyard from *Milton* (London: Chatto and Windus, 1930), p. 277.

28. Baudelaire, *Intimate Journals*, p. 6.

29. Baudelaire, *Selected Writings*, p. 419.

30. Baudelaire, *Baudelaire as a Literary Critic*, p. 124.

31. Baudelaire, *Intimate Journals*, p. 30.

32. Murry, "Baudelaire," p. 96.

33. Jeanne Duval or Lemer (an assumed name, as no one knew her true identity) was a mulatto, sometimes actress, that Baudelaire met toward the end of 1842. She was a great influence on his life; he dedicated a cycle of poems to her in *Fleurs* of which "Le Balcon" and "Un Fantôme" are the most fitting examples.

34. P.M. Pasinetti, "The 'Jeanne Duval' Poems in *Les Fleurs du mal*," in *Baudelaire: A Collection of Critical Essays*, ed. Henri Peyre, p. 92.

35. Jean Prevost, "Baudelairean Themes: Death, Evil, and Love," in *Baudelaire: A Collection of Critical Essays*, ed. Henri Peyre, p. 175.

36. Benjamin, *Baudelaire: A Lyric Poet*, p. 93.

37. Ibid., p. 94.

38. O vierges, ô démons, ô monstres, ô martyrs,
    De la réalité grands esprits contempteurs,
    Chercheuses d'infini, dévotes et satyres,
    Tantôt pleines de cris, tantôt pleines de pleurs, . . .
    "Femmes Damnées," cited in *Flowers of Evil*, ed. Jackson, p. 371. English in text translated by Roy Campbell, cited in *Flowers of Evil*, ed. Jackson, p. 156.

39. Péladan published his novel *L'Androgyne* in 1891.

40. Je croyais voir unit par un nouveau dessin
    Les hanches de l'Antiope au buste d'un imberbe,
    Tant sa taille faisait ressortir son bassin.
    Sur ce teint fauve et brun le fard était superbe!
    "Les Bijoux," cited in *Flowers of Evil*, ed. Jackson, p. 255. English in text translated by David Paul, Cited in *Flowers of Evil*, ed. Jackson, p. 27.

41. Georges Poulet, *Baudelaire: The Artist and His World*, trans. Robert Allen and James Emmons, with biographical commentaries by Robert Kopp (Cleveland: World Publishing Company, 1969), p. 156.

42. Ibid., p. 153.

43. Ibid.

44. Ibid., p. 154.

45. Ibid.

46. "In the poem *Le Chat* a voice 'rises and shimmers *over my darkest depths*'. In another poem entitled *Confession*, remembrance springs *'from the dark depths of my soul.'*" (Emphasis is Poulet's.) Cited in Poulet, *Baudelaire: The Artist*, p. 152.

47. Je suis comme un peintre qu'un Dieu moqueur
Condamne à peindre, hélas! sur les ténèbres; . . .
Cited from the poem "Un Fantôme", *Flowers of Evil*, ed. Mathews, p. 273. English in text translated by Robert Allen and James Emmons, cited in Poulet, *Baudelaire: The Artist*, p. 152.

48. Poulet, *Baudelaire: The Artist*, p. 152.

49. Benjamin, *Baudelaire: A Lyric Poet*, p. 147.

50. Poulet, *Baudelaire: The Artist*, p. 134.

51. Ibid., p. 135–36.

52. Vois se pencher les défuntes Années,
Sur les balcons du ciel, en robes sur années;
Surgir du fond des eaux Regret souriant;
Cited in *Flowers of Evil*, ed. Mathews, p. 414. English in text translated by Robert Lowell, cited in *Flowers of Evil*, ed. Mathews, p. 201.

53. George Ross Ridge, *The Hero in French Decadent Literature* (Atlanta: University of Georgia Press, 1961), p. 13.

54. Ibid., pp. 24–25.

55. Ibid., p. 45.

56. Baudelaire in *Selected Writings*, pp. 303–4.

57. Praz, *Romantic Agony*, p. 102.

58. A.E. Carter, *The Idea of Decadence in French Literature 1830–1900* (London: Oxford University Press, 1968), p. 5.

59. Octave Mirbeau, *Torture Garden (Le Jardin des supplices)*, trans. unknown (New York: Lancer Books, Inc., 1965), p. 84.

60. Mirbeau, *Torture Garden*, p. 25.

61. Ibid., p. 121.

62. Ibid., p. 141.

63. Charles Baudelaire, *Artificial Paradise*, trans. Ellen Fox, Foreword by Edouard Roditi (New York: Herder and Herder, Inc., 1971), p. 36.

64. Ibid., p. 36.

65. Edouard Roditi, Foreword to *Artificial Paradise*, p. xxi.

66. Baudelaire, *Intimate Journals*, p. 56.

67. Ibid., p. 39.

68. Ibid., p. 36.

69. Ibid., p. 56.

70. Arthur Symons, *Charles Baudelaire: Translations of "Les Fleurs du mal," "Petits Poèmes*

en prose," and "Les Paradis artificiels" trans. Arthur Symons (London: The Casanova Society, 1925), p. 284.

71. Isherwood, trans., *Intimate Journals*, p. 42.

72. Baudelaire in *Selected Writings*, p. 425.

73. Ross Ridge, *The Hero in French Decadent Literature*, p. 141.

74. Mirbeau, *Torture Garden*, p. 106.

75. Praz, *The Romantic Agony*, p. 191.

76. Philippe Jullian, *Dreamers of Decadence*, trans. Robert Baldick (New York: Praeger Publishers, Inc., 1969), p. 165.

77. Joris-Karl Huysmans, *A rebours*, p. 53.

78. O miroir!
   Eau froide par l'ennui dans ton cadre gelée,
   Que de fois, et pendant les heures désolée
   Des songes et cherchant mes souvenirs qui sont
   Comme des feuilles sous ta glace au trou profond,
   Je m'apparus en toi comme une combre lointaine!
   Mais, horreur! des soirs, dans ta sévère fontaine,
   J'ai de mon rêve epars connu ta nudité.
   Cited from Huysmans, *A rebours*, Introduction by Havelock Ellis, Illustrated by Arthur Zaidenberg (New York: Illustrated Editions Co., 1931), p. 308. Translator for English in text unknown.

79. "... un baiser me tûrait/Si la beauté n'était la mort ... " Charles Mauron, *Introduction to the Psychoanalysis of Mallarmé*, trans. Archibald Henderson, Jr., and Will McLendon (Berkeley: University of Cal. Press, 1963), p. 116.

80. Ses yeux polis sont faits de minéraux charmants,
   Et dans cette nature étrange et symbolique
   Où l'ange inviolé se mêle au sphinx antique,
   Où tout n'est qu'or, acier, lumière et diamants,
   Resplendit à jamais, comme un astre inutile,
   La froide majesté de la femme stérile.
   "Avec ses vêtements ondoyants et nacrés ... ," Cited in *Flowers of Evil*, ed. Mathews, p. 262. English in text translated by F.P. Sturm, cited in *Flowers of Evil*, ed. Mathews, p. 36.

81. Ross Ridge, *The Hero in French Decadent Literature*, p. 100.

82. Baudelaire, *Intimate Journals*, p. 6.

83. Ross Ridge, *The Hero in French Decadent Literature*, p. 86.

84. Carter, *The Idea of Decadence*, p. 105.

85. Ross Ridge, *The Hero in French Decadent Literature*, p. 26.

86. *Princeton Encyclopedia of Poetry and Poetics*, 1974 ed., s.v. "Symbolism," by Alfred Garwin Engstrom.

87. Charles Baudelaire wrote in his essay on Victor Hugo:"Among the best poets, there are no metaphors, comparisons or epithets which are not adapted with mathematical exactitude to the particular circumstance, because these comparisons, metaphors, and epithets are

drawn from the inexhaustible storehouse of universal analogy and cannot be found elsewhere." Cited in Hyslop, ed. and trans., *Baudelaire as a Literary Critic*, p. 239.

88. Baudelaire in *Selected Writings*, p. 50.

89. Engstrom, "Symbolism," p. 837.

90. John Milner, *Symbolists and Decadents* (London: Studio Vista Limited, 1971), p. 51.

91. Ross Ridge, *The Hero in French Decadent Literature*, p. 57.

92. Bernard Weinberg, *The Limits of Symbolism* (Chicago: University of Chicago Press, 1966), p. 236.

93. Havelock Ellis, Introduction to *A rebours*, p. xiv–xvi.

94. Ibid.

95. Milner, *Symbolists and Decadents*, p. 43.

96. Philippe Jullian, "Dreams of Decadence," *Réalités* 266 (January 1973), p. 16.

97. Milner, *Symbolists and Decadents*, p. 43.

Chapter 3

1. Rainer Crone, *Andy Warhol*, trans. John William Gabriel (New York: Praeger Publishers, Inc., 1970), p. 8.

2. Ibid., p. 10.

3. "I adore America and these are some comments on it. My image is a statement of the symbols of the harsh, impersonal products and brash materialistic objects on which America is built today. It is a projection of everything that can be bought and sold, the practical but impermanent symbols that sustain us." Cited in Lawrence Alloway, *American Pop Art* (New York: Macmillan Publishing Company, Inc., 1974), p. 109.

4. Koch, *Stargazer*, p. 114.

5. Ibid., p. 120.

6. Unpublished taped interview with the filmmaker in 1971. Transcribed by the author in August 1972.

7. Jonas Mekas, "Jack Smith, Or The End of Civilization," *The Village Voice*, 23 July 1970, cited in Jonas Mekas, *Movie Journal*, pp. 393–95.

8. *Andy Warhol*. This book was published on the occasion of the Andy Warhol exhibition at Moderna Museet in Stockholm in February and March 1968. (New York: World-wide Books, Inc., 1970), p. 6.

9. Gerard Malanga, "Interview with Jack Smith," *Film Culture* 45 (1967), p. 14.

10. Hyslop, ed., *Baudelaire as a Literary Critic*, p. 113.

11. Malanga, "Interview with Jack Smith," p. 15.

12. Bergen and Cornelia Evans, *Dictionary of Contemporary American Usage* (New York: Random House, 1957), p. 168.

13. Ibid., p. 168.

14. Gregory Markopoulos, "Innocent Revels," *Film Culture* 33 (1964), p. 42.

15. Jack Smith, "The Perfect Filmic Appositeness of Maria Montez," *Film Culture* 27 (1962/1963), p. 31.

16. Ibid., p. 31.

17. Rex Reed, *People Are Crazy Here* (New York: Dell Publishing Co., Inc., 1974), p. 51.

18. Fran Lebowitz, "All that glitters is not gold, honey," *Changes* 74 (June 1972), p. 1.

19. Ibid., p. 28.

20. Ibid.

21. Stefan Brecht, "Family of the f.p.," *The Drama Review* 13 (Fall 1968), p. 133.

22. Ibid., p. 134.

23. Ibid., p. 120.

24. Ibid., p. 140.

25. Ibid., p. 134.

26. Smith, "Perfect Filmic Appositeness," p. 28.

27. Ronald Tavel, "The Theatre of the Ridiculous," *TriQuarterly*, no. 6 (1966), p. 101.

28. Ibid., p. 101.

29. Ibid., p. 100.

30. Ibid., p. 98.

31. Brecht, "Family of the f.p." p. 139.

32. Ibid., p. 127.

33. Interview with Jack Smith, New York, New York, August 1972.

34. Interview with Jack Smith, New York, New York, August 1972.

35. Jack Smith, "Soundtrack to *Blonde Cobra*," *Film Culture* 29 (1963): pp. 2–3.

36. Unpublished taped interview with the filmmaker, Jack Smith, Anthology Film Archives, New York. Transcribed by the author in August 1972.

37. Ibid.

38. Ibid.

39. Ibid.

40. Markopoulos, "Innocent Revels," p. 41.

41. Jonas Mekas, "*Flaming Creatures* at Knokke-le-Zoute," *The Village Voice*, 16 January 1964, cited in Jonas Mekas, *Movie Journal*, p. 111.

42. Jullian, "Dreams of Decadence," p. 16.

43. Jullian, *Dreamers of Decadence*, p. 11.

44. Ibid., p. 12.

45. Renan, *Introduction to Underground Film*, p. 178.

46. Ibid., p. 178.

47. For a detailed account of the filming of *Normal Love*, refer to Joan Adler's account, "On Location," printed in Dwoskin, *Film Is*, pp. 11–23.

48. Curtis, "English Avant-Garde Film," p. 979.

49. Jullian, "Dreams of Decadence," p. 16.

Chapter 4

1. Jullian, *Dreamers of Decadence*, p. 218.

2. Ibid., p. 220.

3. "A manifesto, written and illustrated by the Surrealists was included in the programme of *L'Age d'Or*." *Classic Film Scripts: L'Age d'Or and Un Chien Andalou* trans. Marianne Alexandre (New York: Simon and Schuster, 1968), p. 7.

4. "In books about the seventh art one often reads that I was influenced by Buñuel, but this is quite absurd, for we shot our films *simultaneously* .... " (Italics mine.) Cited in André Fraigneau, recorder, *Cocteau on the Film: Conversations with Jean Cocteau*, trans. Vera Traill, Introduction by George Amberg (New York: Dover Publications, Inc., 1972), p. 35.

5. Roger Shattuck, Introduction to *The History of Surrealism*, by Maurice Nadeau, trans. Richard Howard (New York: The Macmillan Company, 1965), p. 25.

6. Maurice Nadeau, *The History of Surrealism*, trans. Richard Howard, Introduction by Roger Shattuck (New York: The Macmillan Company, 1965), p. 47.

7. Shattuck, Introduction to *History of Surrealism*, p. 24.

8. Antonin Artaud, *Antonin Artaud Anthology*, ed. Jack Hirschman, trans. David Rattray, "On Suicide" (San Francisco: City Lights Books, 1965), p. 56.

9. Nadeau, *Surrealism*, p. 184.

10. Julien Levy, *Surrealism* (New York: The Black Sun Press, 1936), p. 23.

11. André Breton, *Manifestoes of Surrealism*, trans. Richard Seaver and Helen R. Lane (Ann Arbor: University of Michigan Press, 1969), p. 26.

12. Shattuck, Introduction: *History of Surrealism*, p. 22.

13. "The fact that I myself, at the moment I paint, do not understand the meaning of my paintings does not mean that these paintings have no meaning; on the contrary, their meaning is so profound, complex, coherent, involuntary, that it escapes the simple analysis of logical intuition .... All my ambition, on the plastic level, consists in materializing, with the most imperialistic fury for precision, the images of concrete irrationality." Salvador Dalí, *La Conquête de l'irrationel* (1935), cited in Nadeau, *History of Surrealism*, p. 308.

14. Francisco Aranda, *Luis Buñuel: A Critical Biography*, trans. David Robinson (New York: Da Capo Press, Inc., 1976), p. 67.

15. Herbert S. Gershman, *The Surrealist Revolution in France* (Ann Arbor: University of Michigan Press, 1969), p.31.

16. Raymond Durgnat, *Luis Buñuel* (Berkeley: University of California Press, 1967), pp. 22–38.

17. Ibid., p. 24.
18. Ibid.
19. Ibid., p. 35.
20. Ibid., p. 30.
21. Jack Smith, "Soundtrack of *Blonde Cobra*," *Film Culture* 29 (1963), pp. 2–3.
22. Renan, *Introduction to Underground Film*, p. 152.
23. Sitney, *Visionary Film*, p. 368.
24. Mekas, "On the Baudelairean Cinema," p. 86.
25. Renan, *Introduction to Underground Film*, p. 152.
26. Parker Tyler, *Underground Film: A Critical History* (London: Martin Secker and Warburg, Ltd., 1969), pp. 81–82.
27. Smith, "Soundtrack of *Cobra*," p. 3.
28. "Much more than in any 'mental vantage point,' they found in passionate devotion to a single woman over a long period of time the surest means of liberating desire . . . . The cult of the mythical woman, foreign as it may be to some contemporary readers, lies at the heart of the surrealist credo." Shattuck, Introduction to *History of Surrealism*, p. 25.
29. Jean Cocteau, *Two Screenplays: The Blood of a Poet and The Testament of Orpheus*, trans. Carol Martin-Sperry (New York: The Orion Press, 1968), p. 34.
30. Ibid., p. 53.
31. Ibid., pp. 56–58. [Photographs intervene and separate the text.]
32. Ibid., p. 83.
33. Frederick Brown, *An Impersonation of Angels: A Biography of Jean Cocteau* (New York: The Viking Press, 1968), p. 249.
34. Ibid. p. 299.
35. Ibid.
36. Sitney, *Visionary Film*, p. 33.
37. Lyrics from the song "My Boyfriend's Back," by The Angels (1963), on Smash Records. See Appendix B for publication information on all the major pop songs in Kenneth Anger's films.
38. Tyler, *Underground Film*, p. 15.
39. "An Interview with Kenneth Anger," conducted by *Spider* magazine, reprinted in *Film Culture* 40 (Spring 1966), pp. 69–70.
40. Tony Rayns, "Lucifer: A Kenneth Anger Kompendium," *Cinema* 4 (October 1969), p. 26.
41. Ibid., p. 29.

Chapter 5

1. J.E. Cirlot, *A Dictionary of Symbols*, trans. Jack Sage, Foreword by Herbert Read (New York: Philosophical Library, Inc., 1962), p. 60.

2. Sergei Eisenstein, *Film Form and The Film Sense*, ed. and trans. Jay Leyda (Cleveland: The World Publishing Company, 1957).

3. Peter Wollen, *Signs and Meaning in the Cinema*, (Bloomington: Indiana University Press, 1969), p. 57.

4. Sadoul, Georges, *Dictionary of Film Makers*, ed. and trans. Peter Morris (Berkeley: University of California Press, 1972), p. 7.

5. Sitney, *Visionary Film*, p. 122.

6. Interview with the filmmaker, Berkeley, California, April 25, 1974.

7. John Symonds, Introduction to *The Confessions of Aleister Crowley: An Autohagiography*, ed. John Symonds and Kenneth Grant (New York: Bantam Books, Inc., 1971), p. xiii.

8. John Symonds and Kenneth Grant, *The Confessions of Aleister Crowley*, p. 37.

9. Symonds, Introduction to *Confessions of Crowley*, p. xvi.

10. Ibid., p. xxii.

11. Kenneth Anger at a presentation of his films at the San Francisco Art Institute, April 1974.

12. Ibid.

13. L.W. de Laurence, *The Book of the Sacred Magic of Abra-Melin, the Mage*—As Delivered by Abraham the Jew Unto His Son Lamech—a grimoire of the fifteenth century, translated by S.L. MacGregor-Mathews (former Secret Chief of the Golden Dawn and Head of the Second Order in the Great White Brotherhood, Rosicrucians.) (Chicago: The de Laurence Co., Inc., n.d.).

14. Interview with the filmmaker Berkeley, California, April 25, 1974.

15. Aleister Crowley, *777* (San Francisco: Level Press, no date given), p. 19.

16. Interview with the filmmaker, Berkeley, California, April 25, 1974.

17. From the song "Dream Lover," by the Parris Sisters (1959) on Atco Records. See Appendix B for all major pop songs used in Kenneth Anger's films.

18. Sitney, *Visionary Film*, p. 104.

19. ". . . faced with strange puns and punctuation; with curious syntactical constructions which weave unexpected opposites into daring new patterns; with grim humour continually dissolving ecstatic lyrical flights in a cloud of ambiguities and teasing commas . . . " Alexis Lykiard, Introduction to Isadore Ducasse-Lautréamont's *Maldoror*, trans. Alexis Lykiard (New York: Thomas Y. Crowell Company, 1970), p. vi.

20. Kenneth Anger at a presentation of his films at the San Francisco Art Institute, April 1974.

21. Ibid.

22. Ibid.

23. Sitney, *Visionary Film*, p. 123.

24. Eisenstein, *Film Sense*, p. 231.

25. Rayns, "Anger Kompendium," p. 29.

26. Ibid., p. 26.

27. Eisenstein, *Film Form*, p. 46.

28. Eisenstein, *Film Form*, pp. 78–79.

29. Sitney, *Visionary Film*, p. 116.

30. Ibid., p. 119.

31. Interview with the filmmaker, Berkeley, California, April 25, 1976.

32. Rayns, "Anger Kompendium," p. 26.

33. Interview with the filmmaker, Berkeley, California, April 25, 1976.

34. Rayns, "Anger Kompendium," p. 31.

Conclusion

1. John Milner, *Symbolists and Decadents*, p. 7.

2. Sontag, *Against Interpretation*, p. 230.

3. Arthur Knight, and Hollis Alpert, "The History of Sex in Cinema, Part XV: Experimental Films," *Playboy* 14 (April 1967), p. 136.

4. Ken Kelman, "Smith Myth," *Film Culture* 29 (Summer 1963), p. 5.

5. Baudelaire, "On Hugo," cited in *Baudelaire as a Literary Critic*, p. 239.

6. Baudelaire, "The Governance of the Imagination," cited in *Selected Writings*, p. 306.

Filmography

1. Kenneth Anger, Program Notes for a screening at Pacific Film Archives, Berkeley, California, April 10, 1974.

2. Ibid.

3. Ibid.

4. Tony Rayns, "Kenneth Anger Chronology," Program Notes for screening at the London Film-makers' Coop., 1971.

5. Kenneth Anger, Program Notes for screening, "1970 Magick Lantern Cycle," at the Telegraph Repertory Cinema, October 1970.

6. Rayns, "Anger Chronology."

7. Anger, "Magick Lantern Cycle".

8. Ibid.

9. Ibid.

10. Ibid.

11. Renan, *Introduction to Underground Film*, p. 149.

12. Ibid.

13. Sitney, *Visionary Film*, p. 376.

14. Renan, *Introduction to Underground Film*, p. 149.

15. Ibid.

16. Ibid., p. 207.

17. Sitney, *Visionary Film*, p. 354.

18. Renan, *Introduction to Underground Film*, p. 178.

19. Sitney, *Visionary Film*, p. 377.

20. Sontag, *Against Interpretation*, p. 229.

21. Sitney, *Visionary Film*, pp. 386–87.

22. James Stoller, "Shooting Up," in *The New American Cinema*, ed. Gregory Battcock (New York: E.P. Dutton & Co., Inc., 1967), p. 80.

23. Sitney, *Visionary Film*, p. 123.

24. Ibid.

25. Dwoskin, *Film Is*, p. 214.

26. David Curtis, *Experimental Cinema: A Fifty-Year Evolution* (London: Studio Vista Limited, 1971), p. 152.

27. Descriptions of Warhol's films are taken from Koch, *Stargazer*, pp. 143–51.

28. Ibid., p. 65.

Bibliography

Books

Adler, Joan. "On Location," in *Film Is: The International Free Cinema*. London: Peter Owen Limited, 1975.

Artaud, Antonin. *Antonin Artaud Anthology*. Edited by Jack Hirschman. Translated by David Rattray. San Francisco: City Lights Books, 1965.

Aranda, Francisco. *Luis Buñuel: A Critical Biography*. Translated by David Robinson. New York: Da Capo Press, Inc., 1976.

Baudelaire, Charles Pierre. *Artificial Paradise*. Translated by Ellen Fox. Foreword by Edouard Roditi. "The Taste for Infinity". New York: Herder and Herder, Inc., 1971. pp. 33–37.

_____. *Selected Writings on Art and Artists*. Edited and translated by P.E. Charvet. "The Painter of Modern Life." Baltimore: Penguin Books, Inc., 1972. pp. 390–435.

_____. *Selected Writings on Art and Artists*. Edited and translated by P.E. Charvet. "The Salon of 1846." Baltimore: Penguin Books, Inc., 1972. pp. 47–107.

_____. *Baudelaire as a Literary Critic*. Edited and translated by Lois H. Hyslop and Francis E. Hyslop. "Exposition Universelle 1855." University Park: The Pennsylvania University Press, 1964. pp. 78–84.

_____. *Baudelaire as a Literary Critic*. Edited and translated by Lois H. Hyslop and Francis E. Hyslop. "New Notes on Edgar Poe." University Park: The Pennsylvania University Press, 1964. pp. 114–35.

_____. *Baudelaire as a Literary Critic*. Edited and translated by Lois H. Hyslop and Francis E. Hyslop. "The Salon of 1859." University Park: The Pennsylvania University Press, 1964. pp. 179–86.

_____. *Baudelaire as a Literary Critic*. Edited and translated by Lois H. Hyslop and Francis E. Hyslop. "Théophile Gautier." University Park: The Pennsylvania University Press, 1964. pp. 149–79.

_____. *Baudelaire as a Literary Critic*. Edited and translated by Lois H. Hyslop and Francis E. Hyslop. "Victor Hugo." University Park: The Pennsylvania University Press, 1964. pp. 233–47.

_____. *The Flowers of Evil*. Edited by Jackson Mathews and Marthiel Mathews. New York: New Directions Publishing Corp., 1955.

_____. *Les Fleurs du mal, Petits poèmes en prose, Les Paradis artificiels*. Translated by Arthur Symons. London: The Casanova Society, 1925.

_____. *Intimate Journals*. Translated by Christopher Isherwood. Introduction by W. H. Auden. Boston: Beacon Press, 1930.

Benjamin, Walter. *Charles Baudelaire: A Lyric Poet in the Era of High Capitalism*. Translated by Harry Zohn. London: NLB, 1973.

Breton, André. *Manifestoes of Surrealism.* Translated by Richard Seaver and Helen R. Lane. Ann Arbor: University of Michigan Press, 1969.

Brown, Frederick. *An Impersonation of Angels: A Biography of Jean Cocteau.* New York: The Viking Press, 1968.

Carter, A.E. *The Idea of Decadence in French Literature 1830-1900.* London: Oxford University Press, 1958.

Cirlot, J.E. *A Dictionary of Symbols.* Translated by Jack Sage. Foreword by Herbert Read. New York: Philosophical Library, Inc., 1962.

Classical Film Scripts: L'Age d'Or and Un Chien Andalou. Translated by Marianne Alexandre. New York: Simon and Schuster, 1968.

Cocteau, Jean. *Two Screenplays: Blood of the Poet and The Testament of Orpheus.* Translated by Carol Martin-Sperry. New York: Orion Press, 1968.

Crone, Rainer. *Andy Warhol.* Translated by John William Gabriel. New York: Praeger Publishers, Inc., 1970.

Curtis, David. *Experimental Cinema: A Fifty-Year Evolution.* London: Studio Vista Limited, 1971.

de Laurence, L.W. *The Book of the Sacred Magic of Abra-Melin, The Mage.* Chicago: The de Laurence Co., Inc., n.d.

Durgnat, Raymond. *Luis Buñuel.* Berkeley: University of California Press, 1967.

Dwoskin, Stephen. *Film Is: The International Free Cinema.* London: Peter Owen Limited, 1975.

Eisenstein, Sergei. *Film Form and Film Sense: Essays in Film Theory.* Edited and Translated by Jay Leyda. New York: The World Publishing Company, 1957.

Fraigneau, André. *Cocteau on the Film: Conversations with Jean Cocteau.* Recorded by André Fraigneau. Translated by Vera Traill. Introduction by George Amberg. New York: Dover Publications, Inc., 1972.

Huysmans, Joris-Karl. *A rebours.* Translator unknown. Introduction by Havelock Ellis. New York: Three Sirens Press, 1931.

————. *A rebours.* Translator unknown. Introduction by Havelock Ellis. Illustrated by Arthur Zaidenberg. New York: Illustrated Editions Co., 1931.

Jullian, Philippe. *Dreamers of Decadence:* Symbolist Painters of the 1890s. Translated by Robert Baldick. New York: Praeger Publishers, Inc., 1969.

Kermode, Frank. *Romantic Image.* New York: Vintage Books, a Division of Random House, 1957.

Kitses, Jim. *Horizons West: Anthony Mann, Budd Boetticher, Sam Peckinpah: Studies of Authorship within the Western.* Bloomington: Indiana University Press, 1969.

Levy, Julien. *Surrealism.* New York: The Black Sun Press, 1936.

Lykiard, Alexis. *Lautréamont's Maldoror.* Translated by Alexis Lykiard. New York: Thomas Y. Crowell Company, 1970.

Mekas, Jonas. *Movie Journal: The Rise of a New American Cinema, 1959-1971.* "Jack Smith, or the End of Civilization." New York: The Macmillan Press, 1972. pp. 388-97.

Mekas, Jonas. *Movie Journal: The Rise of a New American Cinema, 1959-1971.* "Flaming Creatures at Knokke-le-Zoute." New York: The Macmillan Press, 1972. pp. 111-15.

————. *Movie Journal: The Rise of a New American Cinema, 1959-1971.* "The Irresponsibility of My Colleague Film Critics, On the Baudelairean Cinema." New York: The Macmillan Press, 1972. pp. 84-86.

————. *Movie Journal: The Rise of a New American Cinema, 1959-1971.* "On Cinéma Vérité, Ricky Leacock, and Warhol." New York: The Macmillan Press, 1972. pp. 153-55.

————. *Movie Journal: The Rise of a New American Cinema, 1959-1971.* "On How the Underground Fooled Hollywood." New York: The Macmillan Press, 1972. pp. 301-2.

————. *Movie Journal: The Rise of a New American Cinema, 1959-1971.* "On the Misery of Community Standards." New York: The Macmillan Press, 1972. pp. 141-44.

_____. *Movie Journal: The Rise of a New American Cinema, 1959-1971.* "The Supreme Obscenity of the United States Congress." New York: The Macmillan Press, 1972. p. 316.

_____. *Movie Journal: The Rise of a New American Cinema, 1959-1971.* "The Year 1964." New York: The Macmillan Press, 1972. pp. 173-74.

Milner, John. *Symbolists and Decandents.* New York: E.P. Dutton & Co., Inc., 1971.

Mirbeau, Octave. *Torture Garden (Le Jardin des supplices).* Translator unknown. Introduction by L.T. Woodward, M.D. New York: Lancer Books, Inc., 1965.

Murry, John Middleton. "Baudelaire." In *Baudelaire: A Collection of Critical Essays*, pp. 94-109. Edited by Henri Peyre. New Jersey: Prentice-Hall, Inc., 1962.

Nadeau, Maurice. *The History of Surrealism.* Translated by Richard Howard. Introduction by Roger Shattuck. New York: The Macmillan Company, 1965.

Pasinetti, P.M. "The 'Jeanne Duval' Poems in *Les Fleurs du Mal.*" In *Baudelaire: A Collection of Critical Essays*, pp. 86-93. Edited by Henri Peyre. New Jersey: Prentice-Hall, Inc., 1962.

Poulet, Georges. *Baudelaire: The Artist and His World.* Translated by Robert Allen and James Emmons. Biographical Commentary by Robert Kopp. New York: The World Publishing Company, 1969.

Praz, Mario. *The Romantic Agony.* Translated by Angus Davidson. London: Oxford University Press, 1933. 1951 edition.

Prevost, Jean. "Baudelairean Themes: Death, Evil, and Love." In *Baudelaire: A Collection of Critical Essays*, pp. 170-77. Edited by Henri Peyre. New Jersey: Prentice-Hall, 1962.

Princeton Encyclopedia of Poetry and Poetics. 1974 ed. "Symbolism," by Alfred Garwin Engstrom.

Reed, Rex. *People Are Crazy Here.* New York: Dell Publishing Co., Inc., 1974.

Renan, Sheldon. *An Introduction to the American Underground Film: A Unique, Fully Illustrated Handbook to the Art of Underground Films and Their Makers.* New York: E.P. Dutton & Co., Inc., 1967.

Ridge, George Ross. *The Hero in French Decadent Literature.* Athens: University of Georgia Press, 1961.

Roditi, Edouard. Foreword. In *Artificial Paradise*, pp. vii-xxii. Translated by Ellen Fox. New York: Herder and Herder, Inc., 1971.

Ruff, Marcel. *Baudelaire.* Translated and slightly abridged by Agnes Kertesz. London: University of London Press, Ltd., 1966.

Sadoul, Georges. *Dictionary of Film Makers.* Edited and translated by Peter Morris. Berkeley: University of California Press, 1972.

Shattuck, Roger. Introduction. In *History of Surrealism*, pp. 11-34. By Maurice Nadeau. Translated by Richard Howard. New York: The Macmillan Company, 1965.

Sitney, Paul Adams. *Film Culture Reader.* Edited and with an Introduction by P. Adams Sitney. New York: Praeger Publishers, Inc., 1970.

_____.*Visionary Film: The American Avant-Garde.* New York: Oxford University Press, Inc., 1974.

Sontag, Susan. *Against Interpretation and Other Essays.* "Jack Smith's *Flaming Creatures.*" New York: Dell Publishing Co., Inc., 1966. pp. 228-34.

_____. *Against Interpretation and Other Essays.* "Notes on Camp." New York: Dell Publishing Co., Inc., 1966. pp. 277-93.

Symonds, John and Grant, Kenneth. *The Confessions of Aleister Crowley: An Autohagiography.* New York: Bantam Books, Inc., 1971.

Symons, Arthur. *The Symbolist Movement in Literature.* Introduction by Richard Ellman. New York: E.P. Dutton & Co., Inc., 1919.

Tyler, Parker. *Underground Film: A Critical History.* London: Martin Secker and Warburg, Ltd., 1969.

Warhol, Andy. No author. New York: Worldwide Books, Inc., 1970.

Weinberg, Bernard. *The Limits of Symbolism:* Studies of Five Modern French Poets. Chicago: University of Chicago Press, 1966.
Wollen, Peter. *Signs and Meanings in the Cinema.* Bloomington: Indiana University Press, 1969.

Periodicals

"An Interview with Kenneth Anger." Conducted by *Spider* Magazine. Reprinted in *Film Culture* 40 (Spring 1966): 87–71.
Brecht, Stefan. "Family of the f.p." *The Drama Review* 13 (Fall 1968): 117–41.
Curtis, David. "English Avant-Garde Film: An Early Chronology." *Studio International Journal* (London) 190 (November–December 1975): 978–80.
Jullian, Philippe. "Dreams of Decadence." *Réalités* 266 (January 1973): 16–21.
Kelman, Ken. "Smith Myth." *Film Culture* 29 (Summer 1963): 4–6.
Knight, Arthur and Alpert, Hollis. "The History of Sex in Cinema, Part XV: Experimental Films" *Playboy* 14 (April 1967): 136.
Lebowitz, Fran. "All that glitters is not gold, honey." *Changes* 74 (June 1972): 1.
Malanga, Gerard. "Interview with Jack Smith." *Film Culture* 45 (Summer 1967): 12–16.
Markopoulos, Gregory. "Innocent Revels." *Film Culture* 33 (Fall 1964): 41–46.
Mekas, Jonas. "A Call For a New Generation of Film Makers." *Film Culture* 19 (Summer 1959): 1–4.
――――. "Notes on the New American Cinema." *Film Culture* 24 (Spring 1962): 6–17.
Rayns, Tony. "Lucifer: A Kenneth Anger Kompendium." *Cinema* 4 (October 1969): 23–31.
Rowe, Carel. "Illuminating Lucifer." *Film Quarterly* XXVII (Summer 1974): 24–33.
Sarris, Andrew. *Village Voice*, 17 May 1976, p. 130.
Smith, Jack. "The Perfect Filmic Appositeness of Maria Montez." *Film Culture* 27 (Winter 1962/63): 28–36.
Smith, Jack and Jacobs, Ken. "Soundtrack to *Blonde Cobra.*" *Film Culture* 29 (1963): 2–3.
Tavel, Ronald. "The Theatre of the Ridiculous." *Triquarterly* 6 (Spring): 93–107.
Tyler, Parker. "For *Shadows*, Against *Pull My Daisy*: An Argument by Parker Tyler." *Film Culture* 24 (Spring 1962): 28–34.

Unpublished Sources

Interview with Kenneth Anger, Berkeley, California, April 25, 1976.
Kenneth Anger Presentation at the San Francisco Art Institute, April 1974.
Interview (on tape) of Ken Jacobs. Anthology Film Archives, recorded in 1964. Transcribed by the author in August 1972.

Index